Source Books on Education
(Vol. 51)
Garland Reference Library of Social Science
(Vol. 1113)

Children's Literature
Developing Good Readers

Edited by
Hannah Nuba
Deborah Lovitky Sheiman
Michael Searson

GARLAND PUBLISHING, INC.
A MEMBER OF THE TAYLOR & FRANCIS GROUP
New York & London
1999

Library of Congress Cataloging-in-Publication Data

Children's literature : developing good readers / edited by Hannah
Nuba, Deborah Lovitky Sheiman, Michael Searson.
p.   cm. — (Garland reference library of social science ;
v. 1113. Source books on education ; v. 51)
Includes bibliographical references and index.
ISBN 0-8153-2395-6 (alk. paper)
1. Children—United States—Books and reading.   2. Children's
literature—Bibliography.   I. Nuba, Hannah, 1924–   .
II. Sheiman, Deborah Lovitky.   III. Searson, Michael.   IV. Series:
Garland reference library of social science. Source books on education ;
vol. 51.
Z1037.A1C496   1999
028.5'3—dc21   98–25543
                                                        CIP

Cover photograph: Tony Donovan, The Ivoryton Studio

Printed on acid-free, 250-year-life paper
Manufactured in the United States of America

Contents

Chapter Twelve

Postscript
Hannah Nuba, Deborah Lovitky Sheiman,
and Michael Searson

Preface

There is always activity in the field of children's literature. Books marketed to children are flooding the shelves of major bookstores and public libraries. Parents and educators have so much choice that often selecting the right children's book can be confusing. This book is a unique approach to sifting through the diverse publications available for children.

The format of this volume helps the reader to gain a global understanding of children's literature in light of children's developmental needs. By providing a better understanding of the abilities, interest,s and maturity levels of children, *Children's Literature: Developing Good Readers* enables parents, teachers, and caregivers to select the most appropriate reading materials. The books mentioned in this volume are classics or timely and relevant contributions to the field of children's literature.

Children's Literature is a reference tool. Each chapter guides the reader through a developmental stage of early childhood and offers excellent examples of appropriate, well-written children's books. Additionally, the essays by award-winning children's author Cari Best and the talented children's illustrator Anita Riggio help the reader understand the process of creating works for children. To create this book the editors used the numerous resources of the outstanding New York Public Library Early Childhood Resource and Information Center. However, *Children's Literature* is national in scope, and the literature noted is available throughout the United States.

The idea for this book reflects the unique contributions of a children's librarian, an educational consultant, and an early childhood professor. However, the talent and commitment of each chapter essayist calls attention to the dedication of all who guide young ter essayist calls attention to the dedication of all who guide young children. It is their vital drive, along with the support of Garland Publishing editors, Marie Ellen Larcarda and Anne Vinnicombe, and the technical assistance of Carol Buell, that made this contribution a reality. Additionally, recognition must be given to the notable work of Julie Cummins, Coordinator of Children's Services for New York Public Library. The New York Public Library Early Childhood Resource and Information Center is the recipient of all proceeds from this volume. It is our hope that the excellent work of those affiliated with the center will continue long into the future.

Hannah Nuba, M.S., Program Coordinator
The New York Public Library
Early Childhood Resource and Information Center

Deborah Lovitky Sheiman, Ed.D.
Educational Consultant
Fairfield, Connecticut

Michael Searson, Ph.D., Professor
Department of Early Childhood and Family Studies
Kean University of New Jersey

Part I

The History and Definition
of Children's Literature

Chapter One
A Brief History
of Children's Literature

Deborah Lovitky Sheiman

In the 1980s the U.S. government set out to prove what most teachers and many parents had suspected, the importance of reading to children. U.S. Department of Education researchers explored what parents of academically successful children do that sets these children apart from their less able peers. Using sophisticated research methods, they found that what works is the most basic of enrichment techniques, reading to children (U.S. Department of Education 1987). Extensive research has revealed that it does not matter whether a family is wealthy or poor; if parents read to their children regularly, starting at an early age, the children benefit from the academic enhancement for years to come. Educators have long contended that parents who foster reading encourage and enhance their children's education. In essence, reading to a child will inspire a child to read.

This commonsense approach to learning success is not new. Before the formal advocacy of early education, Comenius believed that language provided the foundation for all later learning. To further his theory he designed books especially for children. These books appeared in the beginning of the 1600s and are among the earliest specifically made for young people. Johann Pestalozzi, Friedrich Froebel, Maria Montessori, and John Dewey all stressed the importance of reading to children and children's reading. In the United States alone, early children's reading materials ranged from the Bible to adult literature suitable for the young.

Further investigation into the historical and philosophical roots of children's literature has shown that the arrival of printing presses fostered opportunities for children's learning. Printing presses made children's books less expensive. Early primers called hornbooks appeared. These early children's books were usually religious in nature, but secular instruction books that taught the alphabet and hygiene were also common.

The rise of Puritanism in the United States influenced the number of books available for young people. Under the Puritan doctrine children were considered miniature adults in need of salvation. As writings became a means to rescue children from sin, the numbers of books appropriate for children expanded. Instructional volumes customarily contained religious messages and illustrations. Morality, religious obligations, and reverence for God were at the heart of Puritan children's literature. Nonreligious reading materials were thought to be frivolous and the work of the devil.

By the end of the seventeenth century the tide of somber religious writings began to change. Books still familiar today, such as *Mother Goose* (Anderson 1873) and *Little Red Riding Hood* (Perrault 1821) became popular. Chapbooks, the forerunner of contemporary comic books, suited the tastes of the young in the late 1600s. These crudely illustrated and printed action adventure stories delighted children and disturbed adults. Nevertheless, they were as much a childhood favorite of this era as they are today.

In the eighteenth century, writings for children reflected changing perspectives. Children were no longer believed to be miniature adults but to be developing youngsters in need of adult attention and nurturing. Religious instruction ceased to be the primary aim of children's literature. New views on children's maturation promoted books that stimulated the child's sense of fantasy and imagination. Books originally intended for adult audiences trickled down to children.

Literature as entertainment quickly replaced literature as religious instruction. The first major publisher to realize the potential of the children's book category was John Newbery. One of the most notable prizes in children's literature was ultimately named after him—the Newbery Book Awards are still coveted today. Following Newbery's lead, publishing houses opened in major cities such as Boston, New York, and Philadelphia. The number of books intended for the child audience swelled as America entered the golden age of children's literature, the nineteenth century.

The Victorian age of the nineteenth century promoted literature as an amusement and diversion from work, study, or responsibility. Authors of children's literature became famous, and their work is still cherished by children today. The books of Louis Carroll, Kate Greenaway, and Robert Louis Stevenson were and still are outstanding. The fairy tales and folklore of Hans Christian Andersen and the Grimm brothers aroused the child's imagination, while Horatio Alger stories spiritually motivated older children to work hard and succeed. Adventures like *Treasure Island* (Stevenson 1883) and *Alice in Wonderland* (Carroll 1866) filled the pages of children's books. The introduction of science fiction brought such immortal titles as *Twenty Thousand Leagues under the Sea* (Verne 1870). Stories of life in distant countries—like *Heidi* (Spyri 1880) and *Little Lord Fauntleroy* (Burnett 1886)—opened up new worlds to children living in rural and urban America.

Similarly during this period, illustration in children's literature took on importance. Contemporary thought suggests that children's books, especially those written for the very young, are not complete without a visual component. However, illustrated children's books did not become the norm until Randolph Caldecott delighted audiences with his carefree drawings. Today the Caldecott Medal for illustration in children's literature is a revered prize. Even the children's magazine market rocketed in this new era. Publications such as the *Youth's Companion* and *The Riverside Magazine,* both now defunct, provided hours of enjoyable activity with crossword puzzles, stories, and helpful articles.

The innovations in children's literature of the 1800s carried into the twentieth century. Many of the same trends continued and flourished and matured. Library departments developed solely to provide suitable reading materials for the young. A new specialist, the children's librarian, came into existence. Children's literary criticism emerged in 1924 with *The Horn Book Magazine,* published in Boston, which continues today. Similarly during this time, publishing houses hired editors whose sole focus was children's literature.

Wide distribution of inexpensive books helped to establish the popularity of reading. From drugstore racks to grocery store shelves, parents treated their youngsters to the favorably priced and still published Golden Book series. Golden Book subjects ranged from fairy tales to stories about counting elves. For years they have been a source of colorful and well-illustrated reading for the very young. Other ries such as the Bobbsey Twins (Hope 1921), the Hardy Boys (Dixon 1923), and Nancy Drew (Keene 1930) provided pleasurable reading material for school-age boys and girls. Today it is hard to find an American child who has not encountered *The Berenstain Bears* (Berenstain and Berenstain 1964), *The Sesame Street Book* (Children's Television Workshop 1970), or *Where's Waldo?* (Handford 1987). From the sensational stories of pulp fiction to the fantasies of Dr. Seuss, children in the twentieth century have become independent consumers of literature.

The success of children's books has created an industry in itself. In the United States alone, it accounts for over a billion dollars a year. The writing, publishing, and distribution of books appropriate for all children have been helped by groups such as the Council on Interracial Books for Children, the American Library Association, and the Children's Book Council. These organizations have worked to see that there are adequate books available that appeal and relate to the needs of all children in this country. Fictional and nonfictional books celebrate the lives and cultures of diverse peoples. Today, books written about and illustrating minorities are an accepted part of mainstream publishing and reading.

As the twentieth century ends, a second golden age in children's literature has emerged. New categories of children's books abound. From the oversized picture book to the toy book to informational nonfiction series, there are innumerable volumes available to meet the needs and pleasures of all children. Children's literature is an exciting and rewarding aspect of the spectrum of lifetime reading.

The Importance of Children's Literature

Children's literature is a powerful form of communication. Children, like adults, relate to books that give both meaning to their lives and understanding to their daily predicaments. Children eagerly seek out what helps them understand their world, and a good book can do just that.

Each book that a child experiences is an account of an event, whether real or fictional. This event is the veneer. It supplies a medium for the idea behind the story. For example, the story might be about a child's bedtime ritual of being tucked in by his mother, who never leaves the room without first turning on a small light. The message behind this tale is that it is acceptable to be afraid of the dark. Ideas underlying a story can send powerful emotional messages to children who lack the practice and verbal acumen to describe and evaluate their daily experiences.

The messages within a story help children interpret the complicated world as they grow up. Consolidating the messages of a book can provide a child with a fundamental abstract principle or insight that is important both to the story and to life in general. Insight helps children to explore their feelings. In the fear-of-the-dark example used earlier, a child can interpret the principle underlying the story to mean that other children, too, are frightened. The child then comes to understand that it is normal to be afraid of the dark and that he or she will eventually conquer the fear.

The events of a young child's life are analogous to those of a well-written story. Each new event is wonderful and magical or scary and puzzling. Literature offers children the opportunity to rehearse and to relate to the past, present, and future. Whether through the literal interpretation of the story, through the message behind the story, or through the meaning and insight derived from the story, children gain valuable experience interpreting the complex emotions at the foundations of their personal worlds.

Children and adults absorb literature in significantly different ways. Message and meaning may be less conscious for a child who has yet to experience the array of situations that an adult has encountered. Abstractions are still to be formed in the child's mind. Experiences are viewed from a concrete perspective. Occasionally the message and meaning of a story will rest in the back of a child's mind until eventually a new situation brings them to the surface. It is then that the child's own emotional needs match the message and become valuable in bringing meaning to a puzzling dilemma. For this reason an adult frequently finds a moral message in a story, whereas a child interprets the same story literally.

Children react to literature with all the passion of uninhibited emotion. Books are powerful tools in bringing out joy, hate, anger, fear, happiness, envy, love, sorrow, and enthusiasm. A good book can expand a child's horizons, or limit their focus to a single important event or feeling. It can deepen their understanding of others or single out their sensitivities. A good book provides a child the opportunity to relate to a situation, express what they think and feel, and open a new window to the world in which they live. Part of what makes good children's literature so worthwhile is the gentle sensitivity with which it introduces children to the essence of life.

The Importance of Reading to Children

It is hard to doubt the value of a good book. However, few of us ever really contemplate the significance of reading to children. What may appear on the surface to be twenty minutes of retelling someone else's tale can have an effect on a child. Repeating this seemingly unimportant process many times over can have a lifelong impact.

Children are never too young to be read to, nor can nonreaders ever be read to too often. Sharing a book with a young child helps to develop not only literacy and vocabulary, but also an understanding of people and things. Additionally, the bonding that develops between the child and the reader can deepen knowledge, respect, love, and understanding. Since the benefits of reading to a child are so numerous, the following paragraphs will more carefully consider the relationship between reading and literacy development, and reading and emotional development.

Reading and Literacy Development

Literacy problems are besieging our country. The question of why Johnny can't read can be easily answered—Johnny's parents probably never read to him. Young children who are frequently read to seem to grasp the intricacies of reading sooner and comprehend more than children whose caregivers do not read to them. From the cradle to the grave, exposure to books creates a literate and informed person who enjoys and appreciates books.

Similarly, children who enjoy reading and who read often seem to be more successful in language development. Inherent in the process of reading is the learning experience. Repeatedly sharing a book creates exposure to words, and children learn the meaning of words by hearing them in the context of a story. Illustrated books, through visual aid, help further the child's understanding of what he or she hears when being read to.

Books provide opportunities to use words that are not used in everyday conversation. An example is Richard Scarry's illustrated edition of *Mother Goose* containing the familiar nursery rhyme *"Little Miss Muffet"* (Scarry 1988):

Little Miss Muffet
Sat on a tuffet
eating her curds and whey.
There came a big spider
who sat down beside her
and frightened Miss Muffet away.

Rare is the child who has not been exposed to that nursery rhyme. Rarer yet is the adult who commonly uses words like curds and whey in daily conversation. Literature opens the door to vocabulary that is not commonly used but which is easily understood through pictures and context.

Children listen and learn. Hearing groups of words together reinforces the idea of structure in our language. Words together make up sentences. How those words sound to the child suggest whether the sentence is asking a question or exclaiming a statement. What seems so apparent to the adult has yet to be learned by a young child. The easiest way for a child to learn is by hearing the words. The more words that children hear, the more they are able to decipher the finer meanings of their language.

Notwithstanding the child's perception of language experience as a whole, the brain becomes sensitive to how the words sound and are put together. The child develops a sense of syntax; nuances of speech, diction, and tone are more easily perceived from hearing the language and seeing the printed word and illustrations. Books designed specifically for very young children are written to facilitate this learning experience. The words used in a book attract children with their rhythm, repetition, and lilt. This inspires children to ask questions about and to comment on what they have heard, which clarifies and reinforces the message of the book. American poet of humor and verse Ogden Nash embodied this tradition in his delightful children's book, illustrated by Maurice Sendak, *You Can't Get There from Here* (1957). Whether stimulating a child's imagination with mental images of monsters and fairy godmothers, or broadening a child's horizons with reflections of people and customs from a far off place or time, books facilitate the child's language and cognitive development.

Reading and Emotional Development

Emotional development is nurtured by two people reading a book together. The cozy setting of a young child sitting on the lap of a caregiver creates a feeling of personal caring and responsiveness. Children learn to associate this enjoyment with reading. Gaining the undivided attention of a nurturing adult promotes secure feelings and a sense of enthusiasm toward reading and books. Sharing the humor of roly-poly Humpty Dumpty falling off his wall, or imagining ourselves in another person's predicament, opens opportunities for comment and discussion. Communications between adult and child are facilitated. Each new story brings the opportunity to learn something new or to reinforce an old lesson. Rereading an old favorite bolsters the child's feelings of comfort and security. By reading a book together, caregiver and child learn to enjoy each other.

In conclusion, reading to children opens channels of communication that might otherwise be overlooked. It allows children to explore new worlds as diverse as each book that is read. A new perspective lies ahead with each new tale. A familiar story offers the comfort of an old friend, always enjoyed and never forgotten. The cumulative value of reading to children should never be underestimated. It leaves an important lifelong impression in the hearts and minds of children.

References

Anderson, Alexander. *Illustrations of Mother Goose Melodies.* New York: Moreau, 1873.
Berenstain, Stan and Jan Berenstain. *The Berenstain Bears.* New York: Beginner Books, 1964.
Burnett, Frances Hodgson. *Little Lord Fauntleroy.* New York: Scribner, 1886.
Carroll, Lewis. *Alice's Adventures in Wonderland.* London: Macmillan 1866. Boston: Lee and Shepard, 1870.
Children's Television Workshop. *The Sesame Street Book.* New York: Preschool Press, 1970.
Dixon, Franklin. The Hardy Boys (Series). New York: Grosset & Dunlap, 1923.
Handford, Martin. *Where's Waldo?* Boston: Little, Brown, 1987.
Hope, Laura Lee. The Bobbsey Twins (Series). New York: Grosset & Dunlap, 1921.
Keene, Carolyn. Nancy Drew (Series). New York: Grosset & Dunlap, 1930.
Nash, Ogden. *You Can't Get There from Here.* Boston: Little, Brown, 1957.
Perrault, Charles. *The History of Little Red Riding Hood.* Philadelphia: M. Charles, 1821.

Scarry, Richard. *Richard Scarry's Mother Goose*. New York: Golden Books, 1988.

Spyri, Johanna. *Heidi*. Zurich: Perthes, 1880. New York: Random House, 1945.

Stevenson, Robert Louis. *Treasure Island*. London: Cassell, 1883. New York: Lovell, 1886.

U.S. Department of Education. *What Works: Research about Teaching and Learning*. Second edition. Washington, D.C.: U.S. Government Printing Office, 1987, p. 2.

Verne, Jules. *Twenty Thousand Leagues under the Sea*. Paris: Hetzel, 1870. Boston: George Smith and Company, 1874.

Chapter Two
What Makes Good Children's Literature?

Deborah Lovitky Sheiman

Classifying Themes in Children's Literature

A good book can stimulate the imagination, comfort the soul, and put a smile on a sad face. Reviews of children's books indicate that most of the better-written ones include themes that are important to a child's development. The majority of themes fall into one or more of the following classifications: developing aspirations and goals, confronting the trials of everyday existence, or developing a sense of affinity and attachment to others. Other important themes include coping with life traumas, developing self-esteem, being kind to others, perceiving and understanding the world, and understanding the consequences of one's actions. In the following paragraphs these eight classifications are explored in more detail.

Developing Aspirations and Goals

To have a dream and to pursue that dream are as important at age five as at age thirty-five. We discover ourselves and our world by having a goal, taking a risk, and pursuing that goal. When we dream, we imagine what we could be, and taking that chance and pursuing the possibilities takes determination, perseverance, and courage. Through this process children learn that "If it is to be, it is up to me" and that it is normal to be apprehensive about trying to make a dream come true. They also learn that if they do not act to make a dream come true, it will not happen.

Books that stress setting goals and a steadfast commitment to action, such as *Brave Irene* (1986) by William Steig, show disappointments not as unique to the child but as a normal part of living and learning. These books teach children that all of us frequently have to take two steps backward to move three steps forward.

In *Brave Irene*, Irene's mother, a hardworking dressmaker, falls ill while finishing a dress for the princess's ball. Seeing that her mother is too sick to leave the house, Irene tucks her into bed and volunteers to deliver the dress. The weather suddenly turns harsh, and brave little Irene has to fight her way to the princess's palace. At times she feels that she will not be able to make it and that she will surely have to turn back, but somehow she finds the strength to continue her journey. Irene's tribulations and her ability to persevere shape this excellent children's story about developing aspirations and goals.

Confronting the Trials of Everyday Existence

Books that discuss common fears that children regularly face range from stories about imaginary monsters created in the child's mind to stories about going to the doctor. It is important to teach children to challenge these fears, so that they recognize that they are not alone in their feelings and that other children also meet with the same irrational and conflicting emotions. Similarly, they must learn ways of overcoming their fears and how to face them with courage and determination. These stories teach children to differentiate between what is intimidating in their imagination and what is a real danger in their daily life. An example of this type of story is Reeve Lindbergh's 1987 book, *Midnight Farm*.

Midnight Farm, true to its title, is the story of a young child's excursion around his farm at this bewitching hour. The plot focuses around a child's fear of the dark; to ease the child's anxiety, his mother leads him on a special tour of their house and barnyard from dusk till dawn. As the mystery and fright of the night fade, so do the child's fears. The book's presentation is comforting and works well to lessen bedtime apprehension in children.

Developing a Sense of Affinity and Attachment to Others

Books that feature themes about love and caring stress making friends and developing relationships with family members. These books emphasize that everyone cares about themselves, and that it is equally important to care about others. They teach a child how to appreciate a loved one and what actions exemplify this love and concern, and they consider the problems that one encounters in family relationships and friendships. Common topics include ways to show goodwill to a close playmate and actions that express love for a family member. Representative of this type of children's literature is the award-winning *Tucking Mommy In* (1988) by Morag Loh.

This 1988 Notable Children's Book reverses the roles of a mother and her children. When mother is too tired to see her daughters off to the land of nod, sisters Sue and Jenny help their mother to bed. The children demonstrate their concern and compassion for their mother's plight in this beautifully written and illustrated book about family love.

Coping with Life Traumas

This classification recognizes that all living things go through a cycle from birth to death. Understanding inevitable loss, separation, and the resulting sadness is a part of growing up and maturing. These stories show children that at times of sadness and separation, they may feel very lonely and unhappy. Books in this category are helpful to children in learning about this touching, often tearful, yet inescapable part of life. These books frequently present funerals as a way for loved ones to say goodbye, or suggest how memories of an animal or a person who has died can bring comfort. A story that looks at the finality of death or the sadness it brings can be helpful to a child coping with the always difficult emotions surrounding loss and grieving. A prime example of this classification is Margaret Wise Brown's *Dead Bird* (1958).

In this classic book, Brown introduces children to the concept of death. The book's young characters find a dead bird in the park. They give the bird a funeral and burial. Each day they respectfully visit the grave. However, as time passes, so does the memory of the dead bird. Although they still play in the park, they forget to visit the grave. Margaret Brown's well-written book lets children know that it is all right to forget and return to a normal life. It also reminds parents that young children do not firmly grasp the idea of time, and that the time it takes for the heart to heal may be different for a child than it is for an adult. This beautiful story reminds the reader that what might seem like forever to a child seems like only yesterday to an older person.

Developing Self-Esteem

Every child is a special person. Learning to appreciate our own uniqueness is part of developing a positive self-image. Books in this category concentrate on promoting pride, dignity, and self-respect. These books range from concentrating on characteristics that make people extraordinary, like a terrific smile or the ability to excel at a specific activity, to understanding how unique attributes contribute to our individuality. Such books might relate to body integrity, gender, and race as special characteristics that create our singular personalities. An excellent example of this classification is the story *Crow Boy* (1955) by Taro Yashima.

Crow Boy is a sensitively written tale of the young school-age child Chibi, who stands out from his classmates. He does not learn as quickly as his peers. Some children even think of Chibi as slow. However, the other children eventually learn to appreciate him when only Chibi's very special talent can save the day. Chibi then realizes that he too is a very valued and needed person. He and the other children discover that it is acceptable for a person to be different and that we must appreciate others for their individual worth.

Being Kind to Others

Developing empathy and compassion are skills necessary for prosocial conduct. Children need to learn that through their actions they can help another person. Showing kindness and having an unselfish concern for another human being, without the expectation of special privilege or reward, is necessary for positive social interaction. Books in this category show the child that pain or need in another person is often like their own.

These books help to develop the rudimentary ability to put one's self in another's shoes. Through reading such stories the child begins to associate consideration for another human being with the way they want others to treat them. Most readers of children's literature are familiar with books that spotlight the principles of kindness, generosity, cooperation, and sharing with others. A fine example of this book classification is *Jim and the Beanstalk* (1970) by Raymond Briggs.

This modernized version of *Jack and the Beanstalk* presents a new twist to an old tale. The aging giant, not as mighty and robust as in his younger years, is in need of help from the strong and youthful lad Jim. Jim visits the old and lonely giant at the top of the beanstalk and helps him find glasses for his failing eyes, a wig to cover his hairless head, and false teeth for his toothless mouth. Jim's gentle spirit and compassionate nature demonstrate his unselfish concern for others.

Perceiving and Understanding the World

This classification explores the fantasies, appearances, and truths the child needs to understand the world beyond the family. These books attempt to clarify children's perceptions of the world. They encourage investigation of the child's individual environment and society at large.

Not everything the child hears and sees is true, and sometimes the truth can be harder for the child to understand than fantasy. Very young children have a submissive acceptance of what they perceive. As they mature developmentally, they need explanations to understand the concrete workings and concepts attached to their observations.

Children learn to differentiate and interpret the sometimes confusing rules of and roles within their physical and social worlds. Not all explanations make sense to young children who have yet to bridge a cognitive gap in understanding. Logical and factual consistencies can conflict with innate thought processes.

Children's literature in this area may focus on gathering facts and determining what is real and what is illusory. Some books in this category deal with trust, deception, and betrayal. Others differentiate between fantasies and truths. *The Emperor's New Clothes* (Andersen 1949) is a prime example of books in this category.

This ever-popular Hans Christian Andersen tale presents a haughty emperor who comes under the power of two very unscrupulous and devious weavers. They promise to weave him the finest of clothes. These garments are so superior that only a king could wear them, and so exceptional that only worthy subjects can see them. While the dishonest weavers take pay from the emperor and quickly escape, the arrogant emperor parades before the town in his new clothes, which are no clothes at all. This timeless satiric message of self-deception delights both children and adults.

Understanding the Consequences of One's Actions

Books in this grouping are lessons in moral conduct and conscience. The results of rebellious acts and defiant deeds in predictable situations are easily identifiable for young children. These books highlight how a child can cope with or adapt to a contrary situation in a manner that does not have negative consequences for anyone concerned.

The intention of these books is to provide frequent reinforcement and understanding between the child's moral judgment and daily behavior. Through example, children are shown that problem solving is more helpful than headstrong and impetuous actions. Children learn to think for themselves, consider the feelings of others, and follow their conscience. Responsibility for one's actions is key to this book category. An example is *A Big Fat Enormous Lie* (1978) by Marjorie Weinman Sharmat.

A Big Fat Enormous Lie portrays a child's moral accountability. When a little boy decides to raid the cookie jar, his conscience gets the better of him. He envisions himself as a green blob that gets bigger by the moment, or in this case, by the cookie. The more he grows, the uglier he becomes. Only by telling his parents the truth does his outlandish vision of himself disappear.

In point, good children's literature makes for good entertainment. A well-written, finely illustrated book can bring hours of enjoyment to a child. The insight gained from a good story is comparable to a summer storm. It is never the startling bang of thunder that lasts in our mind. It is the lingering sense of wonder at the sight of a colorful rainbow after the clouds have passed. A rainbow is both powerful and amazing, yet suggestive and inspiring. Well-written children's literature leaves us with the same feeling. A good book has important things to say and says them in a way that children will listen to and understand.

Choosing a Good Book for Children

The selection of a good children's book is similar to the selection of a good adult book. In both, the reader is searching for qualities basic to good writing. For an adult scouting the stacks of the library, this search may be as difficult as thumbing through hundreds of children's books or as quick and easy as asking the town librarian for a recommendation. Most communities have experienced children's librarians who are happy to help select a well-written, interesting, and appropriate book. Also, prepared reading lists are often available to facilitate selection. Frequently these lists divide the books by age or grade. Topical lists can be helpful in finding just the right book for a particular occasion.

Stretching a child's imagination through literature kindles creative thought. However, a word of warning is appropriate. Sometimes very young children have a blurred conception of reality and fantasy. Their egocentric thought process colors the boundaries between what is real and what is make-believe. The younger the children are, the more likely they are to perceive fantasy as truth.

Fantasy can be beneficial in that it allows the child to rehearse life events before they take place. Mentally practicing a new or frightening situation enables the child to enter the experience with less anxiety. However, defying the natural role of fantasy and mistaking it for reality can lead to dangerous situations and serious consequences. The fictitious Jack might be able to climb to the top of the beanstalk without repercussions, but little Jimmy should not climb to the top of a tree unsupervised, for he just might fall. It is therefore extremely important to select literature that fits the developmental level of the child and to remind young ones that the story being read is fictitious—an invention of the author's imagination.

Consumers of children's books are aware of the specific qualities inherent in well-written juvenile literature. Any good book, whether written for adults or children, needs convincing, credible characters. Children, like their grown-up counterparts, more readily relate to characters with believable personality traits.

Children's books often use animals portrayed as humanlike in their actions, emotions, and experiences. This is neither peculiar nor confusing to a young child. Although the use of an animal figure represents creative fancy, its given traits must still be convincing. The child must be able to connect with the character. Beatrix Potter's Peter Rabbit stories (first published in the United States in 1934) are still fine examples of animals displaying humanlike idiosyncrasies and traits in a humorous and exaggerated style. Good literature, like Beatrix Potter's, creates memorable characters that juggle the elements of reality, stretch the child's imagination, and provide enjoyable reading for both child and adult.

With a little reminder of what differentiates reality from fantasy, most children are able to understand that people lack phantasmal abilities. Yet, this does not limit children's appreciation of visions like Mary Poppins and Peter Pan. Much of the characterization in books for young children is plainly an exaggeration of specific traits or actions. This portrayal makes the character more engaging and frequently adds a touch of humor to a whimsical persona.

Humor is an important aspect in the majority of children's books. Youngsters delight in the slapstick comedy that propels a character into some form of chaos or exaggerates an otherwise normal situation to extravagant proportions. Incongruity of word, image, or sound is basic to many things young children find funny.

Peggy Parish's well-known *Amelia Bedelia* (1966) is an excellent example. Amelia Bedelia's slapstick humor delights children with a play on words. Housekeeper Amelia follows orders to the tee. She draws the drapes with a pencil and paper. When asked to help prepare dinner by dressing the chicken she ties ribbons and bows around it.

Personification of a concept is recurrent in children's literature. Often books geared to the very young child will characterize a moral issue such as good versus evil or right versus wrong. For example, the familiar theme of the fairy godmother triumphant over the evil stepmother clearly shows the virtues of good prevailing over bad. This clear overstatement is easy for children to understand. It delivers an unquestionable, universal moral message. The classic story of Cinderella is the proverbial example.

A credible character placed in an original concept with a well-devised plot will hold the attention of any young child. Often a good children's book will have a plot so unique that the reader or listener will become absorbed by the very originality of the story. The early Dr. Seuss books share this originality. *The 500 Hats of Bartholomew Cubbins,* written by Dr. Seuss in 1938, is still a fresh favorite. Children become engrossed in the story of an unremovable hat.

A well-written character should have a personality that grows and changes with age and experience. Similarly, there should be a sense of uniqueness that makes the character unforgettable and lifelike. Children should be able to relate to a book's fictional figures.

A good children's book does not exceed the attention span of its intended audience. The brevity, clarity, and compactness of words should correspond to the developmental level of the young child. Within a few sentences the child should learn the necessary facts needed for understanding the plot. Books for youngsters frequently use repetition, refrains, and rhyming to emphasize the story line or important facts. This adds a pleasing sense of simplicity and linguistic lilt. Maurice Sendak's *Pierre, a Cautionary Tale* (1965) has that lilt, repetition, rhyming, and sheer simplistic power.

Children understand that the drama in *Pierre* is playful. The child has an awareness of the action as it happens but is not afraid. Evident is the familiar clash of good and evil, but danger and fear are mocked by Sendak's treatment of easy images, vivid words, and flowing sounds. Sendak's talent imparts an uncomplicated, whimsical, and dramatic quality as the plot unfolds. The nature of the approach reduces anxiety. Additionally, remember that children's books should be read in full at one sitting. They are absorbed as a whole. Consequently, the tensions that might build while reading the story are released by the end.

Selecting good children's literature cannot be discussed without broaching the topic of stereotypes. Unfortunately, in any category of literature, whether written for adults or children, the reader does not have to search long or hard to find rigid, biased perceptions of persons or groups. As adults selecting books for children, we cannot be too careful to avoid books that promote this type of blind prejudice. Children are particularly vulnerable to the harmful power of stereotypes. They have not cognitively or emotionally matured to the point where they can understand maliciousness.

Books make powerful impressions on young minds. Children need literature that accurately portrays their own society and heritage, as well as those of others. Realistic treatment of people and places is fundamental to good literature. All too often and particularly in older literature, it is necessary to look out for misleading and chauvinistic gender portrayals. These can be potentially harmful. Occasionally books use what sounds exotic or strange to catch the reader's attention. Sensationalistic depiction can be damaging. Examples of this type of injurious stereotype include many 1950s stories portraying Native Americans in the Old West. Generations of children have grown up reading tales of savage confrontations between cowboys and Indians. Pictures of teepees and rampaging people wielding tomahawks have reinforced this image.

Even the names given to Native American adults in the children's literature of the 1950s had a demeaning connotation. Often names such as Little Big Foot or Big Red Tomahawk projected a mental image of individuals who were not quite as grown up as their settler counterparts. Men often were portrayed as brutal warriors or brave followers. Women were characterized as unappealing, heavyset, toiling squaws or beautiful young Indian princesses. These books read by children of an earlier era promoted stereotypes and lacked information about the Native American culture.

In the 1990s alone, there has been tremendous growth in the Asian population of the United States. Unfortunately children's literature has not kept up with this swing in our population. Few of the children's books available in our country portray a realistic view of Asian people. The "China Doll" illusion of the too-well-behaved, fragile girl and the myth of the mean, overbearing old "Dragon Lady" still exist in too many books written for young people. Unbecoming stereotypes of sly masters of the martial arts and squinty-eyed, bowing exotic foreigners can still be found. Unfortunately it is difficult to find many children's books that describe being an Asian immigrant child in a multicultural society.

Myths, such as those concerning Native Americans and Asians, have given birth to children's books filled with generalizations and half-truths. Too many children, at a vulnerable age for learning a culturally different perspective, have been taught to mock people of a different race, creed, or color. Characters that fill the pages with platitudes and superstitions do more harm than good to a child's understanding of our diverse world. The planet earth is too small for falsehoods promoted in poorly written juvenile literature. Misrepresentations and stereotypes stifle the minds of children. Good children's literature takes a positive approach. It focuses on what people have in common, rather than what makes them different. This philosophy can help to cross the boundaries of humanity and can lead to a greater understanding of others.

Children are dramatically affected by the attitudes, achievements, and ideas of their culture, and by exposure to diverse backgrounds. During the early childhood years boys and girls become aware that not everyone is alike. Literature works well to familiarize children with the multicultural nature of our country. Remembering that all ethnic and cultural groups contribute to society makes for a more tolerant, peaceful world. Avoiding stereotypes is extremely important if children are to form clear concepts of themselves and others.

A good children's book teaches respect for all people. Never derogatory in tone, it examines universal feelings that people share. All people appreciate happiness and joy, and they suffer through fear and sadness. All people worry about similar things. What is more important, all people want to be respected and treated with care and kindness. Good children's literature should entertain, teach, and reinforce these principles.

Selecting Nonnarrative Children's Literature

Most of this discussion of children's literature has centered on narrative books. A quick trip to a library or book store reveals that there are many forms of children's literature apart from the narrative genre. The shelves abound with books that help teach and reinforce the sight and sound of the ABC's. Using techniques such as rhyming, alliteration, and word play, authors have jingled their way into the minds of children. For example, Maurice Sendak puts a smile on the face of the reader when he explains that G is for getting giggles in his well-known *Alligators All Around* (1962).

Similarly, concept books are simplified teaching tools that hold the reader's attention. Concept books teach numbers, colors, and shapes that help children categorize and see the connection between objects or ideas. Concept books are also written about science. These books focus on animals and insects, the weather, and why things happen.

Books that take a child through an average day at school or a visit to the doctor may appear to be little more than a chronology of events for an adult reader. However, for a young child exploring a whole new world, each step is filled with excitement and trepidation. These books can help prepare a child for a new situation or form the basis for discussion of a recent experience. A youngster finds security in knowing that he is not alone in his curiosity, fears, or encounters.

Selection of nonnarrative books is usually for an intended purpose. They are not likely to be well-worn favorites, read over and over each night. Their appeal lies in their resource value. However, as in any good book for the young and the young at heart, nonnarrative literature has to hold the attention of its reader. Books that are too contrived are often hard to understand. Using humor to enhance these books can make even a dull subject entertaining. Artistic presentation can change the focus from the ear to the eye with creative and well-done illustrations and photography. The use of lines, shapes, colors, and textures can be just as instructive and appealing as the written word.

Selecting quality children's literature should not be a difficult task for the aware consumer. There are a vast number of excellent books available for children of any age. Books are the quickest way to enrich a child's life. They expand the human experience and reinforce the very values and attitudes that we strive to develop in today's youngsters.

References

Andersen, Hans Christian. *The Emperor's New Clothes*. Boston: Houghton Mifflin, 1949. (First American publication of book.)

Briggs, Raymond. *Jim and the Beanstalk*. London: Hamilton, 1970.

Brown, Margaret Wise. *The Dead Bird*. New York: W. R. Scott, 1958.

Dr. Seuss. *The 500 Hats of Bartholomew Cubbins*. New York: Vanguard Press, 1938.

Lindbergh, Reeve. *Midnight Farm*. New York: Dial, 1987.

Loh, Morag. *Tucking Mommy In*. New York: Orchard, 1988.

Parish, Peggy. *Amelia Bedelia*. New York: HarperCollins, 1966.

Potter, Beatrix. *The Tale of Peter Rabbit*. New York: Blue Ribbon Press, 1934.

Sendak, Maurice. *Alligators All Around*. New York: HarperCollins, 1962.

Sendak, Maurice. *Pierre, a Cautionary Tale*. New York: HarperCollins, 1965.

Sharmat, Marjorie Weinman. *A Big Fat Enormous Lie*. New York: Dutton, 1978.

Steig, William. *Brave Irene*. New York: Farrar, Straus & Giroux, 1986.

Yashima, Taro. *Crow Boy*. New York: Viking, 1955.

Part II

Voices of an Illustrator and a Writer

Chapter Three
What Makes an Illustrator an Illustrator?*

Anita Riggio

An illustrator is a vessel, a keeper of images.

I grew up in an Italian American family, and the people who peppered my childhood with love and laughter have had the greatest influence on the characters who romp through the pages of my books.

I was the middle child of five; I have one brother and three sisters. Each of my parents had a horde of siblings, each of whom, in turn, had throngs of children. My mother was a fabulous (and I mean *fabulous*) cook and my father was a generous host, so our home at 63 Carline Drive in Clifton, New Jersey, was the site of most family gatherings.

Those afternoons were spent eating, sipping, and yakking around the dining-room table, which, of course, had been fully extended to accommodate the hungry masses.

There were characters of all sorts around that dining-room table. Uncle Augie, bald, bold, and round as a cue ball, was married to Aunt Alba, who had flaming red hair that she teased and sprayed into a pyramid. Aunt Alba always wore stiletto heels, proof enough to my sisters, our cousins, and me that her feet were permanently shaped like a Barbie doll's. "That's wonderful! Wonderful!" regularly punctuated any conversation we kids had with ebullient Uncle Bob. Aunt Edie, Uncle Bob's wife, was a painter; their house smelled like turpentine and tomato sauce. Uncle Arthur puffed on unfiltered Camel cigarettes and looked on while Aunt Mary taught us to whistle through our fingers. Aunt Ellen was a teacher, and she engaged us with stories of her second-grade students. She was also an accom-

*For my faith-keepers, especially Mom and Dad, Sister Irene Marie, Cloe, Luke, and Roland.

plished, if shy, classical pianist, and on most Sunday afternoons, she could be coaxed into playing a sonatina or two. Afterward, Uncle Jim, my godfather, took a turn at the piano, pulling yellowed sheet music of old-time songs from a worn brown leather briefcase he had brought with him. When all the sheet music was expended, my father took the piano bench and played songs by ear, like "Let Me Call You Sweetheart" and "Good Night, Irene." My cousins and I would wait for the grand finale, "Roll Out the Barrel," which he would sing with a gusto fueled by our delighted dance and laughter.

In the quiet time that would follow the hilarity, I often sat beside Aunt Margaret, who was a retired English teacher, principal, and teacher trainer. As we talked, she would stroke the back of my neck with the softest fingers I had ever felt. It was Aunt Margaret who first told me I had talent as a writer and as an artist.

Sister Irene Marie, O.P., was my art teacher for all four of my high school years at Lacordaire School in Upper Montclair, New Jersey. She filled the art studio with interesting still life and a myriad of art supplies. It was heaven with a classical music sound track. To this day, when I listen to classical music while drawing or painting , I think of her. It was through Sister Irene Marie that I came to consider myself an artist.

Even so, my college years were a jolt. Overwhelmed by college life that, by 1970, had been drained of energy and idealism, I became discouraged as an art major at the University of Hartford. After two years, I became convinced that I was not an artist after all, so I slunk over to the theater department, from which I graduated in 1974.

After graduation, serendipity stepped in, and I became a teacher at the American School for the Deaf (ASD) in West Hartford, Connecticut. It was there that I was introduced to the wonders of children's books by the ASD librarian, Alice, with whom I became great friends. I loved teaching there, becoming fluent in sign language and learning about deaf culture.

Still, after several years, it became apparent to me that I was spending too much time designing my bulletin boards and not enough time correcting papers. It was time to get back in touch with the artist I had been. Remembering the encouraging words of Sister Irene Marie many years before helped to rebuild the confidence I had lost as an art student in college.

By this time, I was married to Roland Axelson, a fifth-grade teacher at the time. In 1978, we had our first child, a daughter, Cloe. Each week, Cloe and I went to the library, where I became friendly with the children's librarian, Linda.

Linda opened up worlds for me by introducing me to the work of wonderful writers and illustrators. There were times when she was so excited by a new book that she would lend it to me before the book had even been processed.

I was still studying in this way when our son, Lucas, was born three years later in 1981. In fact, one day, when I was checking out yet another pile of books, the computer sputtered, nearly spouting smoke. I had one hundred books checked out!

When Luke was four months old, I began making my portfolio in earnest. I knew that art directors and editors would want to see drawings of children and animals in different poses, so I devised a series of pictures showing a boy standing perfectly still with his eyes closed, while his brother, sister, and assorted pets tried to rouse him. My purpose was to show that I could draw a character in repose, as well as characters in action.

I made an appointment with the art director at a large publishing house in New York, and off I went, portfolio in hand. The art director was a very kind, soft-spoken man who took a great deal of time looking through my work. When he came to my series of drawings, he suggested that I make them into a dummy.

I was thrilled, but perplexed. "What's a dummy?" I asked. To his everlasting credit, the man did not skip even a beat. He explained that a dummy is a handmade book, an illustrator's tool to establish not only the pictures but the pace of the book. I thanked him and went home, determined to make my first dummy book.

Well, I did make that dummy, "The Mischief That Martin Made." Over five more years and six more dummies, it evolved into "Wake Up, William!"

On June 12, 1986, as I was on my way out to pick up my children from school, the phone rang. It was Jonathan Lanman, the newly appointed editor in chief of Atheneum Children's Books. He had taken my (latest) dummy to the editorial board, and they had liked it. He was calling to offer me a contract for *Wake Up, William!* It would be published in the fall of 1987.

Needless to say, I was ecstatic. I was beyond ecstatic, I was rapturous, overjoyed, exultant! Besides the birthdays of Cloe and Luke, this was the happiest day of my life! I had not given up, after five long years; I had finally landed a picture book contract.

Sad to say, my mother, a librarian at St. Claire School in Clifton, New Jersey, did not live to see the book published. My first bound copies of *Wake Up, William!* were waiting on our back porch when we returned from her funeral. But the library at St. Claire School always gets one of the first copies of any book I publish.

In the three years that followed, I worked from my home studio in Old Wethersfield, Connecticut, illustrating *The Apartment House* by Julie Schmidt (Abingdon Press), *I Go to Sleep* and *I Eat Dinner* by Margery Facklam (Little, Brown), *Beethoven's Cat* by Elizabet McHugh, featuring several neighbors as character models (Atheneum), and *Hobie Hanson, Greatest Hero of the Mall* by Jamie Gilson, starring my children and their friends as character models (Lothrop, Lee & Shepard). The publication of these books precipitated a grand neighborhood event: a celebration and book signing at Alfred Hanmer Elementary School, our local public school, featuring Old Wethersfield celebs–character models of all ages.

In 1990, I published my second picture book, *Gert and Frieda,* a story of friendship, cheerily illustrated in a bright cartoon style and dedicated to my friend, Alice, whom I had met years before at the American School for the Deaf. In this picture book, I am Gert and the character of Frieda is Alice.

The following year, I began to work with editor Karen Klockner at Orchard Books. After seeing some drawings I had done of my children, Karen asked me to illustrate *Dad Gummit and Ma Foot* by Karen Waggoner.

This is a story of two characters who break off their wedding engagement and do not speak to each other until they are reunited fifty years later by a pair of practical jokes. I loved the text immediately, not only for the story, but because the text was wide open, offering endless illustration possibilities. For example, although the story takes place over a fifty-year span, the precise dates were left up to me.

I decided to set the story in the years between 1885 and 1935, largely for the architecture, decorative arts, clothing, and technological advances during that period. Collinsville, Connecticut, where years earlier I had spent days making sketches for an art school project, would provide the perfect geographical setting. I had a wonderful time doing all kinds of research at the tiny Collinsville Public Library and at the Canton and Connecticut Historical Societies.

To bring the characters to life, I asked the retired minister of Immanuel Congregational Church in Hartford, Connecticut, to model for Dad Gummit and my own mother-in-law to model for Ma Foot. There were lots of giggles as both these wonderful people acted out their hidden crotchety sides!

When all the research was complete and the dummy had been approved, I set about making the watercolor paintings, using the color as visual metaphor. Spring colors represent the characters' youth, fall colors represent their middle age, and winter colors represent their advancing years. Additionally, a critical reader will observe that yellow and violet represent Dad Gummit and Ma Foot, respectively; these two colors dominate the opening spreads, disappear during the ensuing feud, and reappear at the climax.

My next project for Orchard Books was *Coal Mine Peaches* by Michelle Dionetti. This story of the life of an Italian American man, told through the eyes of his granddaughter, was offered to me because the editor thought I would be able to draw on my own family background for the illustrations.

The grandparents' house is the Victorian house that belonged to my own grandparents in Passaic, New Jersey. The model for the narrator was my daughter, Cloe, and the model for Peter, the main character, was my dad. In fact, the reader will be able to spot my entire family in a scene of Easter Sunday dinner. I am the woman in the green dress at the far left. My husband, Roland, is the man in the middle accepting a bowl of meatballs from the grandmother, my mother, who loved to feed him.

At the time this painting was made, my youngest sister, Elissa, and Christian, her husband-to-be, were not yet married. I knew they hoped to have a family, so I painted them both, on the right side of the double-page spread, holding a baby of their own. It was a way to have my whole family in one picture, those deceased and those unborn.

When *Coal Mine Peaches* was published with my watercolor and gouache illustrations, my father, convinced that this story depicted our family history, purchased an entire case of copies. Having served as the model for the main character, he autographed these copies and distributed them to his friends.

Dad found himself again in the pages of *A Moon in My Teacup* (Boyds Mills Press), a story of the miraculous events of a Sunday afternoon before Christmas, as told by the narrator, the second-eldest of four sisters.

This is perhaps the most autobiographical of all my picture books. I am the second of four sisters, as is the narrator. On the way to visit their grandparents on Sunday afternoon, the children sing Christmas carols, just as my sisters and I had done when we were young. After opening a window of the Advent calendar hanging in the dining room, the girls listen to the grown-ups chat about the events of the week, while everyone sips tea and nibbles Grandma's biscotti, just as my sisters and I had done.

While three sisters climb the long, narrow staircase to the bathroom, the narrator tiptoes down the hallway and into the darkened parlor, where she inspects the Christmas village made by Grandpa. Much to her amazement, she finds a family in the village: a man, a woman, a donkey, and a tiny child.

Growing up in parochial schools did have its impact. By second or third grade, I had developed the habit of sneaking off the playground and into the adjacent church. This was not necessarily because I wanted to pray. It was because I was convinced that the statues in the church were moving around during off-peak hours, and I was bound to catch them!

I enlisted the help of models to make the oil paintings for this book, one child for the narrator, children who looked like my younger sisters did, and for a final time, my own daughter, Cloe, who had grown too old to be the protagonist of a picture book, but who is pictured here as the older sister. Dad did double duty as Grandpa and as Papa. There is even a page where those two characters are side-by-side.

Next came *Beware the Brindlebeast*, a retold tale with a Halloween spin of an old woman and the dreaded Brindlebeast, a form-changing trickster. I had never been interested in retelling a story, until I happened across "The Hedley Kew," in *More English Fairy Tales*, by Joseph Jacobs.

This story of a woman and the pranks of a scary form-changer was appealing, but the metaphor I would be able to explore within the story was even more intriguing: The way one confronts one's personal beast has everything to do with the quality of one's life.

Beware the Brindlebeast is set just beyond the boundaries of my own backyard in Old Wethersfield, Connecticut. The character of Birdie is based loosely on my friend Alice of *Gert and Frieda* fame.

Art teachers will be gratified to know that some of us who had to make color wheels in art class actually found it useful. Before I begin a series of illustrations for a new book, I construct my palette based on my selection of two complementary colors.

This color-selection is nowhere more apparent than in *Beware the Brindlebeast*. I had a wonderful time playing with complementary and opposing colors: yellow-orange, red-orange, blue-violet (I did not use blue-green). These paintings were done in oil on heavy watercolor paper. I consider painting to be the reward for all the hard work that precedes it!

Every once in a while, a story lands in my lap like a gift. One ordinary Wednesday morning, Pegi Deitz Shea read an early version of her manuscript to our writers' group. The manuscript, then called "Stitches," concerned a young Hmong refugee child, Mai, and her grandmother. When Pegi finished reading, she looked up for our comments, but none of us could speak for the tears.

Finally, I spoke up and told Pegi that I would love to illustrate her manuscript and asked her if she would consider sending it to my editor. At that time, I was under contract with Boyds Mills Press to illustrate an unnamed picture book, so I knew they were on the lookout for something for me. Pegi sent the manuscript and was given a contract for it, and I was indeed given the job of illustrating it.

But when I had reacted so strongly to the text, I had been responding primarily to a very moving story. Now that I had been given the task of illustrating Pegi's text, I realized I had no concept of the Hmong, their culture, or the refugee camp in Thailand where the story takes place. I found myself paralyzed by the responsibility of accurately representing all of it. Slowly, with research, images came.

Because Mai stitches her own pa'ndau, Pegi and I agreed that the illustrations of Mai's pa'ndau should actually be stitched. As illustrator, I designed the three pa'ndau panels for the book and transferred the drawings to cloth, but we needed a Hmong artist to fill my drawings with stitches. My husband had worked with some Hmong teachers in the Hartford, Connecticut, public school system and soon we were in touch with a pa'ndau artist, You Yang.

You Yang and her family were gracious and helpful in pointing out misrepresentations in Pegi's text and in my dummy. We also consulted Hmong historian, author, and photographer Jane Hamilton Merritt, who was a wonderful guide.

With several revised dummies and reams of photographs in hand, I set about illustrating Mai's story. I chose watercolor as the painting medium, because it is at once fragile and strong, much like the characters of Mai and Grandmother.

Realizing that I needed to build a graphic bridge from pa'ndau to paintings, I borrowed design elements from the quilted borders of pa'ndau that I had seen, and incorporated those elements into the watercolor borders around the larger paintings for the book.

After *The Whispering Cloth* was published, I was invited to speak about it to students at the American School for the Deaf (ASD), where I had been a teacher.

At ASD, I met Mai, a Hmong student who had been born in the Ban Vanai camp in Thailand. (Many Hmong children became deaf in the camps due to lack of proper medical treatment.) I learned that Mai and her father did not communicate with each other, since Mai spoke in English and used sign language, while her father spoke only the language of the Hmong.

Mai's teacher told me that after the book was read to them, before my visit, Mai asked if she might borrow it to share with her father. It is my understanding that *The Whispering Cloth* became the point of their communication. Since then, Mai has published in the school magazine her interview with her father regarding his life in Laos and their new life in America. If no other person were to read *The Whispering Cloth*, I will always believe it found its intended audience.

Something of what I learned from the students during my years as a teacher at the American School for the Deaf is reflected in *Secret Signs along the Underground Railroad*. A seed of the idea for *Secret Signs* was planted during a conversation I had with my father's friend,

Pauline. It was Easter, and Pauline was telling a story from her childhood. At this time of year, she said, she always recalled helping the family of a girlhood friend in the candy store owned by her friend's family in Passaic, New Jersey. (This candy store was around the corner from my grandparents' house at 30 Hoover Avenue, the house depicted in *Coal Mine Peaches* and *A Moon in My Teacup*.) Pauline said they had made all kinds of candy: marzipan, gumdrops, and, of course, chocolate bunnies and eggs.

This started me thinking of my own personal favorite, panoramic eggs, which are shells of sugar sheltering an interior painting or vignette. I thought it would be interesting to somehow incorporate an egg like this into a story, but as every writer knows, having a prop is not equal to having a plot.

I began to wonder about circumstances that would necessitate passing a message inside such an egg. What if the message were a secret? What if it were dangerous? Slowly, I began to imagine circumstances in the days preceding the Civil War that might indeed warrant this sort of message-passing. I began to pound out a first draft.

In the first versions of the story, the protagonist was a hearing child. But the story was not working because there was no compelling reason for passing a message inside a sugar egg. I left the computer and went out to the back porch to think.

Ever since my days at the American School for the Deaf, I finger spell thoughts when I'm sitting idle. So, as I was sitting there, ideas that came to mind flowed through my hand.

The instant I recognized what my hand was doing, my plot problem was solved: The protagonist could be deaf. I was especially happy with the idea because the character's deafness was not a problem that needed to be solved; it was the key that unlocked the solution to the story.

As with *Dad Gummit and Ma Foot, Coal Mine Peaches,* and *The Whispering Cloth,* a lot of research was required to find appropriate artifacts, architecture, and costumes.

All illustrations in any of my picture books are from the perspective of the protagonist—if not the physical perspective, then certainly the emotional one. I think this perspective is particularly apparent in many of the watercolor-and-gouache paintings for *Secret Signs*.

What makes an illustrator an illustrator? Technical facility is important, but that is not all. I think an illustrator is a vessel. An illustrator is a curious student of life, of nature, who hoards all she or he has observed, until specific images flow through the fingers and onto paper, defining that which cannot be defined by words.

Chapter Four
What Makes a Writer a Writer?

Cari Best

When I speak to children in schools around the city, I like to speak to them about passions—both theirs and mine—about music or a pet, writing books or riding bikes, a special person or a collection of colored marbles. I try to nudge gently any dormant passions that lie in wait, for I truly believe that a passionate child (as opposed to a passive child) will grow into a passionate adult—a person who cares.

More often than not, a childhood passion is the precursor to an adult passion, the latter being remarkably similar in many ways (though seemingly different) to what we held near and dear so many years ago.

As a child growing up in Queens in the 1950s, I had no idea that one day I would become a writer. As a matter of fact, when people asked me what I wanted to be, I always answered, "a ballplayer." I thought I was born to play ball.

In those days, every kid in the city played with a small pink rubber ball, embossed with the owner's name, that bounced like nobody's business. The ball, of course, was the legendary "spaldeen"—adapted by the Spalding Sporting Goods Company from the core of its tennis balls. I loved my CARI BEST spaldeen so much that I never let it out of my sight. I ran to stop it before it rolled down the sewer. I jumped to catch it before it landed on the roof. I tried not to play with it near traffic, and I hid it under my jacket whenever the neighborhood bully or dogs lurked nearby.

A genuine spaldeen cost twenty-five cents, which, in those days, meant a lot of babysitting or dogwalking to earn enough money for a replacement. And no kid in her right mind wanted to babysit or walk dogs when she could be playing ball. So I tried especially hard to keep mine safe (although I did manage to lose, on the average, about one ball every week). It was another accepted hazard of living in the city—like noise pollution or air pollution.

With time, my ball came to be a natural extension of myself—like my arm or my finger or my nose. I didn't go anywhere without it. My spaldeen bulged out of the pocket of my dress when I went to school (girls were not permitted to wear pants to school yet), and out of the pocket of my pajamas when I went to sleep. Every chance I got, I played ball—before the school bus came, at recess, and as soon as I came home from school—often for hours at a stretch. I was completely and inconsolably obsessed.

Remarkably, no one ever had to make me practice. I wanted to be the best ballplayer I could be. No kidding. So what if I was a girl? I asked myself, What difference did that make? I could play better than any boy. I played games on the street like hit-the-penny, punchball, stickball, stoopball, and the more ladylike A-my-name-is-Alice. Off the curb and off the wall, over the telephone wires, and over the hedges. Outside with friends and inside alone—much to the horror of my mother, who didn't appreciate the patterns of dirty round spaldeen spots that dotted our walls and ceilings. She tried very hard to get me to be a ballerina. But like all good mothers, mine realized early on that my heart was not in first and second position but on first and second base. And one day she gave up the schlepping by bus and train to dancing school every Saturday. Anna Pavlova would have thanked her from the bottom of her toe shoes.

One of the most difficult things for me as a kid was to sit still in school with that ball in my pocket. I remember holding it, smelling it, squeezing it, and running my fingers over the soft fuzzy rubber—and around the seam across the middle. Even the promise of playing ball held a tremendous amount of excitement for me.

Now, years later, I ask myself, What was it about playing ball that had me so caught up in the game? I come up with the same answer every time. Playing ball made me, a painfully shy, self-conscious kid, feel at best, every bit as confident, uninhibited, and ful-filled as the most well-adjusted kid in the neighborhood. Since I could naturally throw and catch and hit as well as any kid on the block, I was accepted, even chosen first on several occasions, to play in every game. I may have been loath to answer in class or speak on the telephone, but on a playing field or on the street, as long as I had my ball, all my shyness seemed to fade away. Actions speak louder than words, some people say, and in this case, I didn't have to say one word to be a star—which was just the way I liked it.

Sad to say, however, my glory days on the playing field were short-lived. Tomboys of my kind may have been cheered on in street games around the city, but when we got older, we were never encouraged to play ball in school and were never ever invited to try out for any of the boys' teams. We were encouraged to be musical or to dance or act or debate. Thus, reluctantly, I came to the realization as a young teenager, that I would have to relinquish my dream to be a great ballplayer.

But since I wasn't musical (and I shrank if anyone even said the words "dance," or "act," or "debate"), I was stuck—stuck with a great arm, good hands, perfect eye–hand coordination, a lot of free time, and a ton of passion.

I began writing in earnest, for many of the same reasons that I played ball. I was attracted to the rhythm of well-chosen words like I was attracted to the rhythm of the bouncing ball. (Chants like A-my-name-is-Alice may have contributed significantly early on.) I applauded the timing of an event in a well-plotted story like I did the timing of a perfect catch or throw. And I loved the grace of a carefully written sentence as much as I loved the grace of the ball as it sailed through the air.

More importantly, I found I was able to carry my writing around with me like I carried that ball—a security blanket of sorts—never letting it out of my sight. In my pocket, in my shoulder bag, in the saddle bag of my bike, in my suitcase, and under my pillow. To the movies, on the subway, and on vacation. I took my writing everywhere—even to bed.

My pencil and paper became a natural extension of myself—like my arm or my finger or my nose. Every chance I had, I wrote. And no one ever had to make me practice. Sometimes I wrote for hours. I went on record as having the longest journal in my high school's history! I was completely and inconsolably obsessed.

Still a painfully shy, self-conscious young adult, writing made me feel confident, uninhibited, and fulfilled. I found that teachers and friends—and even my mother—encouraged me to write. I was given my own feature column in the high school newspaper, and I was voted the best writer by my peers. This time, written words spoke louder than any actions. How marvelous that I could convey my passions without ever having to say a word. I could be as shy as I wanted to be and still be a star—which was just the way I liked it.

And when no one was looking, I held the paper, smelled it, pinched it, and ran my fingers over the smooth surface. The promise of a blank piece of paper was endlessly exciting to me—just like that ball of long ago.

At this point, I would like to clarify that I didn't just give up playing ball one day and start writing the next. My devotion as a writer—my passion—started the minute I printed my name on that spaldeen; it developed and grew, and is still developing and growing every day of my life.

In second grade, for example, I remember writing a poem about spring. It featured the usual second-grade singsong rhymes, and went something like this:

I see the sun, it's popping out,
And so are daffodils, all about.
Spring is the best time of the year,
For it brings everyone good cheer.

That poem was printed in the *Horace Harding Tattler,* where other P.S. 206ers like me got their starts.

It wasn't until a couple of years later, though, that I really started warming up to writing. One day, when I very likely couldn't go outside to play ball because of bad weather, I wrote what turned out to be a proclamation of sorts to my mother, who, at that time, was far away at work in Manhattan. This is what I wrote, word-for-word, courtesy of my mother, who kept the proclamation for over thirty-five years:

The Institute of Saint Catherine's Home hereby awards this special cer-
tificate to Mrs. Anne Best, and gives her the proud and honorable title of
miracle worker for the miraculous miracle she performed on little Cari,

*a former dweller in our home, until Mrs. Best kindly adopted her and
gave her a respectable place under her own roof.*

Sincerely yours,
Saint Catherine

Adopted? Not me. I made the entire thing up from start to finish.
But my mother, who had a fine sense of humor then, and an even
better one later on, consistently threatened to send me back to Saint
Catherine's if I didn't behave myself.

One incident in particular stands out. In fifth grade I was ex-
cused from penmanship homework because my teacher seemed to
think that I had sufficiently mastered the art of cursive writing. Little
did she know that on that same day I would go home, and in my
idleness, and very best cursive writing, compile a long list of all the
fifth-grade obscenities I could think of, along with a couple of less-
than-charming illustrations. It didn't take long for my infamous list
to come to the attention of my Russian grandmother, who, lucky
for me, couldn't read a word of English, but thought my mother
should have a look at the nice pictures I had drawn.

In junior high I remember squirming through an entire class
devoted to plagiarism—all because of something I had done. Thinking that the summary on the jacket of a book by Ernest Hemingway
had a lot more style and panache than I could ever put into any
book report of mine, I copied it. I thought that if budding artists
were encouraged to copy the old masters, why couldn't budding
authors?

And when an English professor at Queens College read my paper about Charles Dickens's *Nicholas Nickleby* and proclaimed, "You
are a born writer," I thought, for the first time in my life, that I
might have been born to do something else besides playing ball—
that maybe a pencil could feel as good in my hand as that ball had.

My growing up years were fraught with these kinds of examples
of love of language and story. They all contributed toward my initia-
tion, however bumpy, into the very special world of children's books.
And if someone today were to look up at the ceiling of my writing
room, he would see random patterns of dirty round spaldeen spots
because, strange as it may seem, I still need to bounce that ball,
especially when I'm thinking of the next story.

Most of my stories seem to start with a feeling—or sometimes even a smell—that I remember from my childhood. For months, I'll carry the feeling around with me while I walk, wash my car, or work in the garden. I'll think about it, sleep on it, and write parts of it in my head, giving it every chance to grow and flourish.

If the feeling is strong enough, it always develops itself into a story. Then, little by little, the characters take shape. Mostly, they're parts of people I know and parts of people I make up. When the story becomes ripe for writing, I try to piece together a plot. But most times, the plot I start with is not the plot I end with. One thing is certain, though: The feeling is the same as the one I first felt.

Here is an example. Once when I was a kid, I saw a dead mouse. It was lying outside Gail Rosenberger's basement window like a rock or a wad of chewing gum or a common clump of dog stuff. It was the biggest dead thing that I'd ever been so close to. It was much bigger than a dead fly or cockroach. I felt revulsion, nausea, awe, and curiosity all at the same time. The mouse made me think of my father, who was the biggest dead thing I'd ever heard of, but didn't know much about.

Every day for a week, I came back to look at the dead mouse. Once I got up the nerve to turn him over with a stick. I studied the stiffness of his tiny ears and feet. I gasped at what had come out of his tiny body and the thousands of ants that were devouring his flesh. Is this what happened to my own father when he died, I wondered. At last I understood why my mother didn't like to talk about him. Or did I?

Years later, when I wrote *Taxi! Taxi!,* I tried to bring my father back, to tell him how much I loved him as I had always wanted to, to get that ride in his yellow taxi as I had always wanted to, to ask him where he was when I kept waiting and waiting for him to come and see me—as I had always wanted to. For me those strong feelings of death and earth and longing kept the story alive.

Oftentimes, in my books, I will use my power as a storyteller to make something positive from something gray and grim. If certain events did not play out happily in my life, those very same events might now play out happily in my stories. *Taxi! Taxi!,* for example, is the story of a young girl who gets to spend a glorious day in the country with her beloved father. He returns her love unconditionally, and promises more sweet times together—even though he must deliver her back to her mother at the end of the day. The universality of the ache and emptiness created by the reality of one parent living elsewhere most probably is felt deep in the hearts of children everywhere. I still feel it.

Red Light, Green Light, Mama and Me was born out of the feeling of love and warmth and security that overwhelmed me each time I stood next to my mother when we traveled by subway. I always knew that come heat or high water, monster or madman, nothing and no one in the whole world (certainly not in New York City) would ever harm me as long as my mother was there. What soon followed was her image, looking so beautiful and so important, as she left me each day to go to work, while I, helpless little being that I was, had to stay behind and cry over her picture. But never again! In my story, Lizzie, an enchantingly bold and charming little girl (much more like my daughter than like me), gets to spend an entire day with her mother at work—not behind a heavy gray metal desk like my mother's, but at the dynamic Downtown Children's Library, where Mama is part of an energetic team, a real "work family" that makes new and exciting things happen every hour!

Getting Used to Harry started with a smell. For me it was the loathsome, lingering, stale smell of cigar associated with a loathsome, lingering, stale person who was very much a part of my childhood. The hard part for me was to find the good in this character, and at the same time provide children in a similar situation with a way to cope—again, to create something positive out of something seemingly hopeless. When Cynthia's mother marries Harry, her home becomes his home, and there is absolutely nothing she can do to change that. There must be an awful lot of Cynthias out there who are having to get used to an awful lot of Harrys. The fact that Cynthia is a child and Harry is an adult is secondary. After all, who would disagree that we would all be a lot better off with a little less bellyaching!

Interestingly enough, the smell of the real Harry's cigar carried me through the writing of the book (although an actual cigar never appears in the story). I never got used to the smell, and, therefore, could not convincingly persuade Cynthia to get used to it either.

Being in touch with what I felt as a child has never been difficult for me; the challenge has been to convert those feelings, however ill and negative, into something that would help a child deal with similar situations in his or her life today.

Something children always find amusing is that despite the fact that I grew up wearing other kids' clothes, most notably a neighbor's (Ellen Katz's embossed underwear, blouses, shorts, and dresses), I had a strong sense of who I was and what I could and couldn't do. I knew that I liked hot dogs and not hamburgers. I knew that I liked the color red and not the color green. I knew that I liked stories about families and that I hated stories about monsters. I knew that if I wanted to I could make myself run fast in a race, spell all the words correctly on a spelling test, and not eat one more bite of liver or I would throw up. I wasn't very interested in science, and I didn't care very much about what I wore. I hated wearing galoshes in the rain, and I hated being sent to bed when it was still light outside.

Understanding who I am helps me in my writing. Sometimes after I've toiled over something for months, I'll read it over and come to the conclusion that I can do better still, or I'll admit that this is the absolute best that I can do, even though the writing might leave much to be desired.

I try to avoid topics I don't care much about. If it doesn't matter to me, then why will it matter to children? I always hope that readers will care as much as I do, even if the story is about *my* grandmother and not theirs—and how much I loved her knees and her cheeks and the sound of Russian. I try to awaken in each of them a passion for my passion—whether it's for playing ball, a dog named Pansy, a puny parrot, a walk in the city, or a ride in a taxi. And, of course, when a child then feels inclined to indulge the passion in himself or herself, I am rewarded. There goes a child who, one day I hope, will grow up to be a caring adult.

Finally, I find that I write best when I am free to write about whatever moves me. I don't write well when the subject is dictated or prescribed. How true, then, that the best things in life are like the best things in writing—free . . . free . . . free.

Part III

Developing Good Readers

Chapter Five
Encouraging Early Reading

Hannah Nuba

In today's world it is universally understood that "the ability to read is among our most vital survival skills" ("C.Q.Researcher" 1995).

Compelling research findings show that children will eventually acquire adequate reading skills in school, but that it is in the home where learning to love reading takes place. And the parent, as the child's first and most influential teacher and lifelong anchor, plays a central, leading role in this process. In fact, parental involvement in the child's growth toward literacy is the single most meaningful indicator pointing to success.

A seminal study by Durkin (1966) shows that the home environment plays "the key role in affecting early achievement." The report found nothing unusual about children who were early readers, except that they were read to by parents who themselves enjoyed reading. These children were also given opportunities early on to become "scribblers" and "paper and pencil kids," as they explored the writing–reading link.

Current thinking continues an expanding definition of reading to encompass all the stages in the child's development on the way to literacy: "Learning literacy is now seen as a continuous process, which begins in infancy with exposure to oral language, written language, books and stories. It is a process that has its roots in the home, with branches extending to other environments" (Strickland and Morrow 1989).

Indisputably, it is the literacy-rich home that provides the fertile ground for growing early, eager readers. "Children who live with adults who cherish books and reading . . . inherently follow these role models by becoming early, enthusiastic readers" (Nuba, Searson, and Sheiman 1994).

The most authoritative, up-to-date study on literacy, "Reading Literacy in the United States," reports that parent involvement not only influences the early years, but spills over into the child's later academic life. "In elementary school with high levels of parental involvement, children do better in reading comprehension; other things equal, 4th grade average reading scores are 26 points below the national average where involvement is low but 17 points above the national average where parent involvement is high"(U.S. Department of Education 1996, p. 7).

Parental involvement in the child's literacy learning begins even before the baby is born. Expectant parents should prepare and furnish the nursery with a "Baby's First Bookshelf" filled with colorful board books.

Newborns find themselves in a world filled with multisensory images and perceptions. They respond with their whole being to a smiling face, reassuring arms, the gently spoken word, and the soothing sounds of lullabies, language-play, and nursery rhymes. Almost from the start, infants show interest in the sturdy, appealing board books just right for looking at, holding, listening to, and a bit of tactile exploration. And as book and baby's mouth meet, the caregiver might ponder the long-ago observation made by Bacon (1561–1626) that "Some books are to be tasted, others to be swallowed, and some few chewed and digested." Of course, Bacon did not have board books and babies in mind, but we know that children exposed to books and being read to in infancy will, as they become adults, reflect on, chew over, and digest more scholarly, esoteric tomes.

As babies grow into toddlers, their appreciation for picture books and stories grows with them. "Read me a story" is a frequent request, as the child snuggles book and self into the cozy lap of a loving adult. Young children adore books about familiar experiences and are beginning to connect the story with the printed symbols and bright illustrations on the page.

This is the ideal time for taking the child to the library. The New York Public Library presents delightful toddler programs, all resounding with songs, rhymes, fingerplays, and age-appropriate books.

Nearly every branch library has a Children's Room for children to age twelve, offering picture books, children's magazines, records, audiocassettes, and, in many branches, microcomputers. There are also wonderful storytelling hours, puppet shows, films, craft and poetry workshops, and music and dance performances.

The New York Public Library also is home to ECRIC (Early Childhood Resource and Information Center). As one of the nation's first and largest libraries dedicated to early childhood development and education, ECRIC serves parents and teachers with a 12,000-volume book and materials collection, as well as workshops, lectures, and seminars.

By age two, the child should be going to the library regularly. At this stage of development the child will benefit greatly from partaking in a storytelling hour. Two-year-olds have developed a strong command of the language and take much pleasure in verbal interaction and pretend reading and writing. Just having come into their preoperational period of growth, they are very concrete in their thinking, not ready for stories with subtle plot lines, abstractions, and fine distinctions. They adore being read to and love picture books with recognizable illustrations or photographs and stories about things they know about.

Wordless books too are a good way to foster a child's creativity and imagination and to help develop a love of language and story. Some are quite sophisticated and are meant for older children, while others are perfect for the very young. For children who have just crossed the magical threshold into the "reading" world, chapter books are favorites. They are easy-to-read stories arranged in short chapter format, charmingly illustrated, often part of a series, with the content interesting and far-reaching enough to captivate newly independent readers.

It is important for parents to understand that children's reading development varies and that the key to raising an avid reader is the reading–enjoyment connection. It is wise not to be judgmental of the books that children choose. Children in the first grade and up find absurd characters and situations hilarious, and the more ridiculous and gross the stories, riddles, and jokes, the better.

Even older children who like to read may, for a time, select only books about their favorite subject or activity, such as sports or horses. Many children are addicted to the R.L. Stine Goosebumps series, while others love comics. Parents and caregivers can relax! Studies show that while some of these selections may not qualify for distinguished literature, they provide reading practice and encourage the habit of reading.

All children deserve to get to know high-quality literature—the classics, poetry, and traditional folk and fairy tales—and nothing is better and more helpful in developing their interest in fine books than reading aloud to children.

In the book *For Reading Out Loud!* (Kimmel and Segal 1983) the authors explain how this simple book-sharing activity enriches children's lives and encourages literary development. The landmark study *Becoming a Nation of Readers: The Report of the Commission on Reading* (Anderson et al. 1995) concluded that "the single most important activity for building the knowledge required for eventual success in reading is reading aloud to children" (p. 23). Jim Trelease, a well-known reading specialist, in his *Read-Aloud Handbook* (1995) teaches adults the techniques and rewards of reading aloud to children. Another important book stressing the importance of reading aloud to children is *Read to Me: Raising Kids Who Love to Read* (Cullinan 1992). Written by Bernice E. Cullinan, an internationally acclaimed educator, the book is filled with step-by-step, hands-on activities "that lead children to read and ways to keep them reading."

Magazines are an additional resource to encourage reading. The expanding number of magazines for preschoolers, school-age children, and preteens shows how popular they have become. Children can borrow magazines from the library, or if they are able, they can subscribe. Children love to receive mail, and when it's a cherished magazine, the pleasure is doubled.

Joining a book club is a positive "spark plug." Book club selections range from preschool to school-age, are less expensive than in the bookstore, and are generally of good quality both in content and construction. Of course kids eagerly await the regular arrival of the books they helped select for themselves—a sure way to get into the reading routine. Newspapers, too, encourage reading interest, as children observe how important the daily newspaper is to the adults in the family. Many newspapers include a section especially for kids, where word and writing games, comics, puzzles, jokes, and poetry are featured. Goldstein and Goldstein (1992) see newspapers as much more than a source of information and entertainment for adults. For children, "Newspapers can be a great springboard for a multitude of educational ideas," and "Emergent readers can benefit from the simple letter searches and shape activities, while older children can practice word skills, learn new vocabulary, and improve their reading comprehension."

Television viewing should be a shared experience for parent and child. With a caring adult at the child's side, even the very young can learn to be aware television watchers. Older children can become discriminating program selectors based on examples set by parents. Programs such as *Mister Rogers' Neighborhood* and *Sesame Street* do promote learning, and the outstanding *Reading Rainbow* for older children was specifically designed to use the medium of television to bring books and children together. Daniel R. Anderson, in "Television and Children: Not Necessarily Bad News" (*The Brown University Child Behavior and Development Letter*, 1989), asserts that "we have little research basis on which to generally indict television as a medium. . . . [It is] our responsibility to monitor the content that the medium brings to our children, for only through monitoring . . . the programs our children watch can we be sure of positive benefits."

Today, however, the advent of the videocassette recorder has become a great boon for parents in their endeavor to find good television programs for their children. They can now easily make excellent choices as they prescreen, before selection, the many videos available for young children. The best among them are closely based on outstanding picture books. These videos are expressly designed to delight young children and to evoke a lifelong appreciation for the power and beauty of language, literature, art, and music.

Reading begins at home, and literature is the link to literacy. Children who have early exposure to the spoken word, written language, books, and stories will acquire a broad set of skills that will lead to early reading, later academic school success, and a lifetime of love for books and reading.

References

Anderson, Daniel R. "Television and Children: Not Necessarily Bad News." *The Brown University Child Behavior and Development Letter*, Vol. 5, No. 9, pp. 1–5. Providence, R.I.: Manisses Communications Group, September 1989.

Anderson, Richard C., et al. *Becoming a Nation of Readers: The Report of the Commission on Reading.* Washington, D.C.: U.S. Department of Education, 1995 "C.Q. Researcher." *Congressional Quarterly,* Vol. 5, No. 19, pp. 441–464. Washington, D.C.: Congressional Quarterly, May 1995.

Cullinan, Bernice E. *Read to Me: Raising Kids Who Love to Read.* New York: Scholastic, 1992.

Durkin, Dolores. *Children Who Read Early: Two Longitudinal Studies.* New York: Teachers College Press, 1966.

Goldstein, Bobbye S. and Gabriel F. Goldstein. *Newspaper Fun: Activities for Young Children.* Carthage, Ill.: Fearon Teacher Aids, 1992.

Kimmel, Margaret Mary and Elizabeth Segal. *For Reading Out Loud! Guide to Sharing Books with Children.* New York: Delacorte, 1983.

Nuba, Hannah, Michael Searson, and Deborah Lovitky Sheiman. *Resources for Early Childhood: A Handbook.* New York: Garland, 1994.

Strickland, Dorothy S. and Lesley Morrow, eds. *Emerging Literacy: Young Children Learn to Read and Write.* Newark, Del.: International Reading Association, 1989.

Trelease, Jim. *The Read-Aloud Handbook.* Fourth Edition. New York: Penguin Books, 1995.

U.S. Department of Education, National Center for Education Statistics. "Reading Literacy in the United States: Findings from the International Association for the Evaluation of Educational Achievement (IEA) Reading Literacy Study." Washington, D.C.: U.S. Department of Education, 1996.

Chapter Six
Babies and Books

Jill Sheiman
Laura Sheiman

Do babies need books? What are the benefits of reading to a baby? Books and babies go together. Books provide new sounds, pictures, and expressions that enrich development. Three and a half centuries ago, Aristotle reminded parents that babies need more than food, clothing, and shelter. To be a good parent also requires being a good teacher.

Books and Milestones of Early Development

By the first birthday celebration, emerging physical, social, and cognitive skills are evident. Immature response patterns discernible at birth have developed into meaningful well-differentiated behaviors. Within their first year babies grow from their newborn size to about one and a half times their height, and three times their weight. They change from tiny infants to active little people with the newly found coordination to creep, crawl, and drink from a cup.

They no longer sleep most of the day but have settled into a pattern of two or three naps a day and a long, uninterrupted night's rest. Eating has changed to a routine two meals and two snacks a day. Erupting teeth cause temporary discomfort but consequently enable the baby to experience a whole new world of adult food. Crying, babbling, and cooing give way to a limited but growing vocabulary of first words, as babies learn to discriminate sounds during the second year of life. The onset of toddlerhood brings a new sense of autonomy and independence. *Busy, Busy Toddlers* (1987) by Phoebe Dunn explains by example the most notable feature of toddlerhood, the child's activity level.

As children become more aware of their surroundings, initial attempts to control the environment lead to more self-assertion and occasional outbursts of emotion and temper tantrums. The toddler's energy keeps Mother and caregiver close at hand. Babies enjoy the nearness of their special persons. They are more receptive to familiar people and objects than to strangers. They have come to understand that Mother is a being separate from others. It is reassuring for them to know that the person who responds to their every need is consistently available. As babies begin to seek independence, they might stray a few feet from their mothers, but they often check to see that Mother is still near. Eventually this pattern gives way to more mature behaviors that satisfy the need for closeness to the object of attachment, while allowing for more independence. The Caldecott Honor Book and Notable Children's Book of 1990, *"More, More, More" Said the Baby: Three Love Stories* by Vera B. Williams, is an endearing reminder of the social skills babies develop in infancy and toddlerhood.

Babies' growing desire for independence can create some less-than-pleasant situations for those responsible for their care. As infants grow into toddlers, they begin their push toward autonomy but still crave the closeness of the first year of life. Routines such as feeding that were once pleasurable for adult and child may now become trying.

It is not unusual for babies to decide suddenly that they no longer like the same foods that just a week or two earlier were favorites. Babies can become quite contrary in the same situations in which they had been previously cooperative. Learning to feed oneself is more than a lesson in nutrition. More food may end up on the floor than in the mouth as babies delight in their new abilities to grasp, drop, and explore the food they eat. The adventures of Max and his sister in *Max's Breakfast* (Wells 1985) is a highly appealing book for this stage in the child's development.

As babies seek out their surroundings they investigate anything and everything discovered along the way, including those things that elicit stern no's. Parents and caregivers should accept this as a part of maturation. Although the manner in which the adult responds to any specific action of the child is not likely to be remembered, it does set a model for how the child learns to react to the world. In *Just Like Daddy* (1981) Asch shows how children imitate those they love. Ainslie Pryor's *The Baby Blue Cat Who Said*

No (1988) is a good story for a time in life when the word "no" takes on new importance.

One area that often presents difficulty for the family is bedtime. Infants do not fight being put to bed. However, as infancy gives way to toddlerhood, sleep routines become continually more difficult. Toddlers do not want to miss out on activity. If they go to sleep, they might miss opportunities to explore something new. No matter how tired, toddlers will rarely volunteer to go to bed. This is an ideal time to use books to help little ones establish satisfying daily routines that ease the tension of bedtime. Reading to children relaxes them so that a comfortable, stress-reduced presleep state can be reached. Similarly, as babyhood gives way to toddlerhood children become more sensitive to the moods and feelings of those who care for them. Through reading, parents can set a quiet mood that helps the baby reach a relaxing presleep state. *Sleep Tight* by B.G. Hennessy (1992) and *Sleepy Book* (1988) by Charlotte Zolotow are excellent bedtime helpers.

The first year of life is the prelingual, or the prelanguage, phase. Babies begin to comprehend concepts and relationships long before they have developed a speaking vocabulary. Each new word learned becomes a symbol of a particular concept. For example, in Fran Manushkin's *The Best Toy of All* (1992) every man the child sees is called "dada." Dada stands for daddy, but it also becomes the category of all men. Each symbolic word empowers very young children with new communication skills. As toddlers mature, the understanding needed for this receptive language gives way to speech, or expressive language.

The more experience babies have with words—using them and hearing them in context—the more enriched the language learning. Hearing the words puts a label on things and concepts. It also helps children to grasp grammatical structure. Reading books to babies enriches this experience and promotes a better understanding of each new label. Truly this is a situation where a picture is worth a thousand words of description. Babies have more adequate foundations to learn and use words if they have a clearer comprehension of what the word is, means, or symbolizes. The adventures of toddler rabbit Max in *Max's First Word* (Wells 1979) is an example of a welcome book fitting this stage in the child's development.

The reaction of others to the toddler's new words can subtly affect the child's future responses and development. The adult response, as perceived by the child, is echoed in his or her later actions and motivations. For example, parents might excitedly respond to their child's first attempts at saying "baby," by lovingly showing Baby his or her photo and cooing "pretty baby." These parents are setting a positive tone about how their children should feel about themselves. Their words and actions are sending a message that Baby is a valued, important human being. This fosters a sense of self-esteem and social growth.

Books at this stage, such as *Baby around the Clock* (Slegers 1987), are likely to have few words and many big, colorful pictures. Parents are able to introduce their own values and beliefs in how they relate to each picture. Babies respond to the reader's tone and imitate the reader's emotional reactions. Facial expressions, sounds, and gestures are picked up by young children and are likely to be copied. Parents can send messages of pleasure and satisfaction or convey anger and annoyance in reaction to pictures and illustrations. Reading books to babies is one of the earliest ways to introduce family values.

Along with spoken language, books introduce babies to the sounds of our language. The "baa" sound of the sheep in *Moo, Baaa, La La La* (1995) by Sandra Boynton is a babbling sound reproducible during the first year of life. Sparsely worded picture books not only further development, but the traditional chants, repetition, rhymes, and lilt of songs and poems are favorites. Familiar verses like "Patty cake, patty cake, baker's man," condition ears to the native language and entertain babies at the same time.

As the normal maturational process unfolds, books become an enjoyable tool to enrich development. Books are a means to open and to share communications with babies. They further the bonding process and forge the relationship. As babies grow older, interactions with the reader and the book change. Passivity gives way to active involvement, and words and pictures take on new meaning. How babies are introduced to books determines their consequential enthusiasm for this important source of developmental stimulation.

Introducing Babies to Books

Parents often wonder if there is a right time or a proper way to introduce babies to books. The answer is that anytime is the right time. The proper way is limited only by book choice and the tender loving attention of the reader. Adult readers are aware that fiction for grown-ups differs from the make-believe stories read to young children. Although the elements of fantasy, imagination, and invention are integral to both, children's stories are woven in a more basic manner.

The explicitness and brevity of children's books allow for easy understanding and reading in a single session. Plots are less complicated. The simplicity of word choice introduces babies to new words and reinforces those already known. The language of the story is written to enrich and strengthen children's natural patterns of language acquisition.

The very brief, basic nature of children's books sometimes makes them the hardest books to write. Communicating the story line is often more difficult to do in a few sentences than in a few hundred pages. Selecting well-written books is essential for enjoyment. Children are much more likely to find pleasure in literature and learning if books are presented as a positive, pleasing experience.

Reading children's stories with expression and gusto makes them more realistic and exciting than a monotoned recitation of words. Parents need never fear the critical ear of the listening child. Young children are not listening to grade their parents on oral reading ability. Children enjoy the lilt of the words, the drama of the illustrations, the special time shared with an adult, and the attention focused on them alone.

Books That Babies Like

Nursery rhymes top the list of first introductions to literature. What baby has not smiled over the rap of *"Patty Cake,"* or laughed at the tales of *Mother Goose*. Babies respond to the cadence and rhyme, even if they lack the experience and maturation to understand the meaning of the verse alone. The beat of the words and the attention of the caregiver can stimulate an interest in books.

Over the course of the first two years of life, babies become increasingly aware of their environment. The bright colors of illustrations attract their eyes. The feel of different textures fascinates their fingers, and the sounds of life intrigue their ears. That is why the first books we buy for babies are usually big picture books, touch and feel books, and interactive play books that emit sounds when pressed.

Some baby books are made to withstand the less-than-kind but good-natured handling of little hands and uncoordinated fingers. These books are printed on heavy-duty paper, cardboard, or vinyl. They are made to resist the effects of sticky fingers, spilled water, and many falls from strollers and high chairs. Although many of these books may have only a word or two and/or a picture on each page, they communicate the idea that books are an enjoyable experience.

Babies learn that pages are for turning, and that pictures represent ideas and words. A good book with a solitary illustration on each page can speak louder to a young child than a book with many words. Caldecott Award winner Maurice Sendak epitomized this with *Where the Wild Things Are* (1963), an almost no-text picture book about Max, who is sent to his room for acting "like a wild thing." Max fantasizes about going to where the wild things live. He dreams of being king of the hill, but in reality Max is safe in his comfortable home.

Such books support the notion that the baby's world is predictable and secure. Repetition supports simple educational concepts and reinforces experiences commonly shared by babies. For example, Sarah Garland's book *All Gone* (1990) reenacts mealtime. *The Baby's Catalogue* (1982) by Janet and Allen Ahlberg depicts the everyday activities, objects, and people that compose a baby's existence.

Humor is regularly found in picture books. Often illustrations might be comical or whimsical. *Old Mother Hubbard* (1984) by Colin and Jacqui Hawkins is entertaining not only in the description of what Old Mother Hubbard has in her cupboard but in the marvelously funny pictures hidden under lift-up flaps.

The very young should also be exposed to artistic beauty. A prime example is the illustrations by Kandy Radzinski in *Lullaby* by Jane Chelsea Aragon (1989). Beautiful watercolors meet the eye while the story tells of a mother's song floating in the wind over hills and woods and water. The charm of this story promotes an aesthetic sense. Foundations are laid for the concepts of color, form, shape, and medium. Children are never too young to learn to appreciate beauty. Repeated exposure to artistic depictions of age-suitable material in picture books encourages aesthetic pleasure.

Similarly, babies delight in interactive action books such as those that make noise, talk, or move. Their participation transforms the object into an interactive toy. Concepts become more real as youngsters practice newly found enjoyment in feeling unique textures, sticking their fingers through holes in the page, and lifting flaps. These books provide an arranged environment where the story comes to life through the child's actions. The movable parts in books like *The Little Engine That Could: A Pop-Up Book* (Piper 1984) and *Pat the Cat* (Hawkins and Hawkins 1983) capture the delight of young children while they reinforce enthusiasm for reading.

Additionally, alphabet and counting books are usually among the first in a baby's library. *The Berenstains' B Book* (Berenstain and Berenstain 1971) and *C Is for Clown* (Berenstain and Berenstain 1972) are examples of books that help children to develop an awareness of words. Hearing and seeing the names of letters directs curiosity to the written word. Finding the humorous examples of each letter in the alphabet help to capture the youngster's very limited attention span.

Counting skills that reinforce concepts of number are well presented in books such as *Fun with Numbers* (Muldoon and O'Brien 1992). The authors present photographs of bibs, toys, and other objects common to babies' daily existence. These pictures are perfect for acquiring elementary counting competency. Similarly, other children's authors have fostered the concept of natural numbers through comical verse whereby farm animals are counted from one to ten and then are counted again, in reverse. Fun verses such as these are an enjoyable way to build the concepts of ordering and numbers, the foundation of mathematical learning.

Children in the first years of life enjoy books, and one of the best ways that caregivers can cater to this enjoyment is to read to babies at every opportunity. Beginning books are especially important in influencing later reading preferences and habits. Vocabulary is heard and used in a context important to understanding. Sentence structure and the style of the writing intuitively familiarize babies with how words are spoken, the length of word groups, sentence structure, and question formation. Babies do not need formal lessons in grammar and word structure to learn the details of their language. They need books and a caring adult. Reading to babies fosters a knowledge of language and the development of future literacy skills.

The enjoyment of babies' first books is a mind-stretching experience. Creativity and the imagination are given free rein. Knowledge of life yet to be experienced is gained through reading. What has been experienced is reinforced through reading. One of the greatest gifts a baby can receive is to be read to often. It is the path to a lifelong habit of reading.

References

Ahlberg, Allen and Janet Ahlberg. *The Baby's Catalogue*. Boston: Little, Brown, 1982.
Aragon, Jane Chelsea. *Lullaby*. San Francisco: Chronicle, 1989.
Asch, Frank. *Just Like Daddy*. Englewood Cliffs, N.J.: Prentice-Hall, 1981.
Bass, Agnes. *A Parent's Treasury*. New York: A.S. Barnes, 1961.
Berenstain, Stan and Jan Berenstain. *The Berenstains' B Book*. New York: Random House, 1971.
Berenstain, Stan and Jan Berenstain. *C Is for Clown*. New York: Random House, 1972.
Boynton, Sandra. *Moo, Baa, La La La*. New York: Little Simon, 1995.
Dunn, Phoebe. *Busy, Busy Toddlers*. New York: Random House, 1987.
Garland, Sarah. *All Gone*. New York: Viking, 1990.
Hawkins, Colin and Jacqui Hawkins. *Old Mother Hubbard*. New York: Putnam, 1984.
Hawkins, Colin and Jacqui Hawkins. *Pat the Cat*. New York: Putnam, 1983.
Hennessy, B.G. *Sleep Tight*. New York: Viking, 1992.
Manushkin, Fran. *The Best Toy of All*. New York: Dutton, 1992.
Muldoon, Eileen McCarney and Mary Bennett O'Brien. *Fun with Numbers*. New York: Maxwell, 1992.
Piper, Watty. *The Little Engine That Could: A Pop-Up Book*. New York: Platt & Munk, 1984.
Pryor, Ainslie. *The Baby Blue Cat Who Said No*. New York: Viking, 1988.
Sendak, Maurice. *Where the Wild Things Are*. New York: Harper & Row, 1963.
Slegers, Guusje. *Baby around the Clock*. New York: Barron's, 1987.
Wells, Rosemary. *Max's Breakfast*. New York: Dial, 1985.
Wells, Rosemary. *Max's First Word*. New York: Dial, 1979.
Williams, Vera B. *"More, More, More" Said the Baby: Three Love Stories*. New York: Greenwillow, 1990.
Zolotow, Charlotte. *Sleepy Book*. New York: Harper & Row, 1988.

Chapter Seven
Children's Literature for the Preschool Years

Michael Searson

The preschool years present a magical and enchanting time during the life of the child in the exploration of children's literature. The years three through five are a period when the child's imagination soars. The inner workings of the child's mind are rich with fantasy, wonderment, and bewilderment. With an independence that language, symbolic representation, walking, and control of their bodily functions has recently brought, children now are struggling with their place in the world, grappling with their role in the family, attempting to forge an identity of their own—all within the comfortable space of their home. Of course, these struggles present many conflicts for the three- to five-year-old. Over the years, good children's literature has provided an outlet for these conflicts to be explored, if only on a subconscious level. Authors of quality preschool children's literature have demonstrated, at some level, awareness of what works best for this age group.

Developmental psychologists have described the preschool years as a period when the growing child attempts to forge an identity appropriate within the confines of acceptance in the family. This exploration is often an internal one where the child demands both independence from and security within his or her family. For example, Erik Erikson depicts the preschooler of this age as pitted in a struggle between initiative and doubt. Erikson has characterized the initiative children display at this age as having "the quality of undertaking, planning, and 'attacking' a task for the sake of being active and on the move" (Erikson 1963, p. 255). Of course, when dealing with these dynamos, there are times when an adult must step in and prohibit certain behaviors that may be deleterious to the child or to others. When the adult does intercede to thwart a child's actions, the child may experience doubt. For it is during this period that the child, with newly acquired motoric and linguistic autonomy, is expected to exhibit behavior appropriate to the responsibilities that this independence brings. For example, a child who takes the toys from the toy box will be expected to put them away and is thus caught in a struggle between these newfound tools of independence and the limits placed upon him or her within the household. Children's literature can provide a forum for this internal conflict. Young children can readily identify with Max in *Where the Wild Things Are* (Sendak 1963), who, when he (rudely) announces his independence from Mom, must (at a subconscious level) rule the wild things, who behave for him just as he would like them to. Or, as with the main character in *Alexander and the Terrible, Horrible, No Good, Very Bad Day* (Viorst 1972), the young child can feel totally frustrated with the complex world around him and just want to escape (to Australia, as Alexander desires). Of course, children's anguish is resolved when they master a messy situation and come to the rescue such as the mouse who saves his father from the trap in *Whose Mouse Are You?* (Kraus 1970).

Perhaps the most orthodox portrayal of the preschooler in psychological conflict comes from Sigmund Freud, whose theory of child development presents the preschooler as one who, at the deepest inner workings of the mind, is struggling with intense psychosexual conflicts. It is during the preschool years, Freud argues, that the young child is sexually attracted to the parent of the opposite sex. This attraction leads the child, at a subconscious level, to plot the death of the same-sex parent. Ultimately, this Oedipus complex is resolved when the child abandons the plan to take the place of the same-sex parent and "chooses" to identify with that parent. Although Freudian psychology is out of favor today, the Bruno Bettelheim classic work on children's literature still resonates. In *The Uses of Enchantment* (1977), steeped in Freudian psychology, Bettelheim argues that repressed sexuality and inner conflict are the bases for all fairy tales. In fact, Bettelheim reasons that the need to address these repressed psychoanalytic feelings has led to the universal fairy-tale formula that, from culture to culture, and using different characters and settings, addresses common needs of young children. For example, in *Little Red Riding Hood,* Bettelheim reasons, the young girl, manifested with a lingering Oedipus complex, is experiencing puberty and menstruation. Whether children do find fairy tales as a subconscious outlet for unresolved Freudian conflicts continues to be debated. In any case, many researchers have made it clear that the themes evident in the most popular fairy tales are universal and can be found in many cultures across the world. Suffice it to say that, for whatever reason, these tales are popular throughout the world and seem to fill some need.

At the cognitive level, Swiss psychologist Jean Piaget contends that major characteristics of the preoperational are symbolic representation and intuitive thinking. For Piaget, language development is evidence of the more general achievement of symbolic thought. That is, children can now represent their world internally, using symbols. These symbolic representations can take many forms, including words (language), dramatic play (acting out), drawing (or other graphic arts), building (e.g., block play), and so on.

Another approach to cognitive development is presented in the work of Lev Vygotsky. Vygotsky (1978) contends that intellectual development takes place within the context of social interaction, particularly between the child and the parent or more advanced peer. This interaction, which ultimately leads to increased intellectual development, occurs within what Vygotsky refers to as the "zone of proximal development." Interactions through children's literature will often create a zone of proximal development. Shared reading experiences can provide powerful examples of Vygotsky's zone of proximal development. Very often when a parent or an older sibling reads aloud to a preschooler, the level of the literature will provide an intellectual encounter that challenges the young child. For instance, when reading *Goldilocks and the Three Bears*, a parent might discuss differences among small, medium, and large sizes. Or a teacher might ask a child why the nameless little boy's solution to the problem in *Mike Mulligan and His Steam Shovel* (Burton 1939) was the most appropriate one. Thus, within the literary zone of proximal development, preschoolers acquire important knowledge about their world.

In recent years, psychologists have extended Vygotsky's zone of proximal development and introduced the concept of scaffolding (Wood, Bruner, and Ross 1976). Through scaffolding, the child and adult (or more capable peer) interact with each other in a manner that progressively increases the child's cognitive development. For example, when reading *Anno's Counting Book* (Anno 1977), the parent can ask the child to count the items on each page. The child who has reached the ability to count low numbers may indicate this by saying, "Let's go to the next page." In this way, the parent can now challenge the child with higher numbers. Because each side can raise the intellectual "ante," we have the so-called scaffolding effect. For preschool children, shared reading experiences are one of the most common ways that scaffolding occurs.

Linguistically, preschool children are characterized by a period of unparalleled language development. Their vocabulary increases from about 200 words as a two-year-old to well over 2,000 words as a five-year-old, who may now be entering kindergarten. (The early school years, including kindergarten and the primary grades, are marked by a continuation of flourishing vocabulary development.) As early preschoolers (about three years old) move along on the road of language acquisition, they often "play" with these newly obtained tools—called words. For example, the young preschooler may often engage in repeating words, and even nonsense syllables and phrases such as, "Me go. We go. Bo, Bo. Go, Mo." This metalinguistic activity represents the child's burgeoning knowledge of and experimentation with this new thing called language. Suitably, for the early preschooler, books that also "play" with language are received with great satisfaction and enjoyment. For example, books such as *Millions of Cats* (Gag 1929) or *Green Eggs and Ham* (Dr. Seuss 1960) that use repetition of words and phrases are greatly enjoyed by preschoolers, who usually join in and repeat the phrases along with the storyteller. Stories with nonsense syllables, or those that use polysyllabic words in refrains, such as *Tikki Tikki Tembo* (Mosel 1968) and "Rikki-Tikki-Tavi," (Kipling, 1894, 1964), also bring much pleasure to children of this age. Playing with language is also a primary characteristic of the Mother Goose nursery rhymes that have fascinated young children over the years. "Hickory, Dickory, Dock," "Pease Porridge Hot," "Peter Piper," and "This Is the House That Jack Built" are examples of nursery rhymes that allow children to play with language.

A primary ingredient in preschoolers' literary experience is their inability to read to themselves. Children at this age will often pretend to read to themselves, using visual cues (e.g., pictures) and memory as guides. In some cases, the older preschooler may even recognize a few words and indeed read them. But, on the whole, children's books for preschoolers are best enjoyed when they are read by someone else. This is usually done by a parent in the home or a teacher in the preschool setting. These literary experiences are often intimate ones that may shape a fondness for literature and reading for the remainder of the child's life. Thus the context within which preschoolers experience literature itself carries psychological undertones. Within such a context it is appropriate that books which focus on intimate images, settings, and themes, such as the family, the child's room, and the child's imagination are among the most popular for preschoolers. Can there ever be a bedtime story richer than *Goodnight Moon* (Brown 1947)? And for the times children find it difficult to fall asleep due to characteristic nighttime fears, there are books like Russell Hoban's *Bedtime for Frances* (1960). Or how about the reassuring mother who guarantees unconditional love in *The Runaway Bunny* (Brown 1942). Then there is the closeness and warmth of the Mallard family in *Make Way for Ducklings* (McCloskey 1941). Beyond the psychological sustenance provided to children who are read to, an additional benefit is derived from reading aloud. Research indicates a positive correlation between those children who are read to and those who go on to become readers (Clark 1976; Cohen 1968; Cullinan, Jaggar, and Strickland 1974; Durkin 1966; Price 1976; Teale 1984). In other words, children who are read to most likely become effective readers themselves.

In the Piagetian model, preschool children are in the cognitive stage referred to as "preoperational" (ages two to seven). Piaget has characterized this stage as one of intuitive thinking, where children are governed by how things appear rather than by the innate qualities of the objects themselves. Thus, for the preschooler, the illusion that the moon is following them as they ride along in a car takes on the semblance of reality rather than illusion. Although as adults we, too, may agree that the moon appears to be following us, our advanced cognitive operations would lead us to understand that it is no more than an illusion. Indeed, relative to our individual movement, the moon remains fixed. Thus, for young children, the world is a magical place where experiences are sometimes a product of their imagination. This is one reason why books of fantasy provide timeless joy to preschoolers. *The Garden of Abdul Gasazi* (1979) by Chris Van Allsburg (or many of his other books), *King Bidgood's in the Bathtub* (1985) by Audrey Wood (illustrated by Don Wood), and *Have You Seen My Duckling?* (1984) by Nancy Tufari are good examples of children's fantasies by contemporary authors and illustrators.

Preoperational children are also characterized as "egocentric" by Piaget. The egocentric child perceives the world from his or her perspective and has difficulty taking on the viewpoint of others. So in *The Snowy Day* (Keats 1962) children are engrossed by a story that represents the experiences of a single character as he explores his world on a snowy day. As children's perspective broadens, they come to understand that there is a whole world out there, comprising many people, all of whom have their own feelings and experiences. As the preschooler decenters (becomes less egocentric) he or she is most fascinated by the world that is most immediate—family, home, neighborhood. However, fully developed decentering does not occur until the child reaches the school years, ages six to twelve. Therefore, preschoolers prefer books that celebrate the world that they know best, which includes the family, home, and neighborhood. Books that identify body parts or common objects that children can see in the home or outside their door or in the neighborhood such as *Richard Scarry's My First Book* (1986), *Richard Scarry's The Best Word Book Ever* (1963), George Zaffo's *The Big Book of Real Trucks* (1950), and Tana Hoban's *Shapes, Shapes, Shapes* (1986) and *Is It Red? Is It Yellow? Is It Blue?* (1978) are among the favorites of preschool children. Books like Rosemary Wells's "Max" books, such as *Max's Bedtime* (1985), and *When You Were a Baby* (1982) by Ann Jonas, which are set in a warm household, tap into the basic needs and security that children of this age require (Maslow 1968).

When it comes to moral development, Lawrence Kohlberg has argued that the behavior of preschoolers is primarily governed by external agents such as rewards and punishment. Preschoolers are, therefore, fascinated by children whose behavior has created situations where rewards or punishment are presented. Mostly these reinforcers are introduced by adults, usually a parent. So when Max in

Where the Wild Things Are (Sendak 1963) is punished by his mother, he can now be the one who doles out rewards or punishment to the wild things in the kingdom where he is the master. Of course, there is the mischievous Curious George, in the series by H.A. Rey, who gets in trouble from the very first book, *Curious George* (1941), when he meets his human owner, and is even arrested. In fact, George manages to get into trouble in the remainder of the books in this delightful series. Or in the classic tale *The Three Billy Goats Gruff* (Galdone 1973), the troll and the billy goats are pitted against each other in a classic confrontation between good and evil. These books make it quite clear that if you misbehave, you will be punished. On the other hand, in classics such as *The Little Red Hen* (Galdone 1973) or Aesop's *The Ant and the Grasshopper* (see Untermeyer 1965), the message is clear: you will be rewarded for good and industrious behavior. Preschool children accept these conditions of reward and punishment as governing principles in their own behavior.

The preschool years may offer the most magical and enchanting times in the enjoyment of good children's literature for both the child and the adult. Whether a teacher of preschool children or a parent at home, readers will remember this period as a time when children attained the cognitive and linguistic ability to understand appropriate literature. It truly is a charming time in the lives of young children, and a special time for those wise enough to take the time to read to them. Stories read to children at this age can resonate for a lifetime. One of the most enduring and meaningful rituals of the preschool years is being read to at bedtime by a parent, or at school by a teacher. After all, perhaps the most special request that a preschool child could make of an adult is "Read it to me, again!"

References

Anno, Mitsumasa. *Anno's Counting Book*. New York: Crowell, 1977.

Bettelheim, Bruno. *The Uses of Enchantment: The Meaning and Importance of Fairy Tales*. New York: Vintage, 1977.

Brown, M.W. *Goodnight Moon*. Illustrated by Clement Hurd. New York: Harper & Row, 1947.

Brown, M.W. *The Runaway Bunny*. Illustrated by Clement Hurd. New York: Harper & Row, 1942.

Burton, Virginia L. *Mike Mulligan and His Steam Shovel*. Boston: Houghton Mifflin, 1939.

Clark, M.M. *Young Fluent Readers*. London: Heinemann Educational Books, 1976.

Cohen, D. "The Effect of Literature on Vocabulary and Reading Achievement." *Elementary English, 45,* 1968, pp. 209–213.

Cullinan, B., A. Jaggar and D. Strickland. "Language Expansion for Black Children in the Primary Grades: A Research Report," *Young Children, 29,* 1974, pp. 98–112.

Dr. Seuss. *Green Eggs and Ham.* New York: Random House, 1960.

Durkin, D. *Children Who Read Early.* New York: Columbia University Press, 1966.

Erikson, E. *Childhood and Society.* New York: Norton, 1963.

Flournoy, V. *The Patchwork Quilt.* New York: Dial, 1985.

Gag, Wanda. *Millions of Cats.* New York: Coward-McCann, 1929.

Galdone, P. *The Little Red Hen.* Minneapolis: Seabury Press, 1973.

Galdone, P. *The Three Billy Goats Gruff.* Minneapolis: Seabury Press, 1973.

Hoban, R. *Bedtime for Frances.* Illustrated by Garth Williams. New York: Harper & Row, 1960.

Hoban, T. *Is It Red? Is It Yellow? Is It Blue?* New York: Greenwillow, 1978.

Hoban, T. *Shapes, Shapes, Shapes.* New York: Greenwillow, 1986.

Jonas, Ann. *When You Were a Baby.* New York: Greenwillow, 1982.

Keats, E. *The Snowy Day.* New York: Viking, 1962.

Kipling, R. "Rikki-Tikki-Tavi." In *The Jungle Book.* Original publication 1894. New York: Doubleday, 1964.

Kraus, Robert. *Whose Mouse Are You?* Illustrated by Jose Aruego. New York: Macmillan, 1970.

Maslow, A.H. *Toward a Psychology of Being.* Second edition. Princeton, N.J.: Van Nostrand, 1968.

McCloskey, R. *Make Way for Ducklings.* New York: Viking, 1941.

Mosel, A. *Tikki Tikki Tembo.* Illustrated by Blair Lent. New York: Holt, Rinehart, and Winston, 1968.

Price, E. "How Thirty-seven Gifted Children Learned to Read." *The Reading Teacher, 30,* 1976, pp. 44–48.

Rey, H.A. *Curious George.* Boston: Houghton Mifflin, 1941.

Scarry, R. *My First Book.* New York: Random House, 1986.

Scarry, R. *Richard Scarry's The Best Word Book Ever.* Racine, Wisc.: Western, 1963.

Sendak, Maurice. *Where the Wild Things Are.* New York: Harper & Row, 1963.

Teale, W.H. "Reading to Young Children: Its Significance for Literacy Development." In H. Goelman, A. Oberg, and F. Smith (eds.), *Awakening to Literacy.* Portsmouth, N.H.: Heinemann Educational Books, 1984.

Tufari, Nancy. *Have You Seen My Duckling?* New York: Greenwillow Books, 1984.

Untermeyer, L. (ed.). *Aesop's Fables.* Illustrated by Alice and Martin Provensen. New York: Golden Press, 1965.

Van Allsburg, C. *The Garden of Abdul Gasazi.* Boston: Houghton Mifflin, 1979.

Viorst, Judith. *Alexander and the Terrible, Horrible, No Good, Very Bad Day.* Illustrated by Ray Cruz. New York: Atheneum, 1972.

Vygotsky, Lev. *The Mind in Society: The Development of Psychological Processes.* Cambridge, Mass.: Harvard University Press, 1978.

Wells, R. *Max's Bedtime.* New York: Dial, 1985.

Wood, Audrey. *King Bidgood's in the Bathtub.* San Diego: Harcourt Brace Jovanovich, 1985.

Wood, D., J. Bruner, and S. Ross, "The Role of Tutoring in Problem Solving." *British Journal of Psychology, 66,* 1976, pp. 181–191.

Zaffo, G. *The Big Book of Real Trucks.* New York: Grossett and Dunlap, 1950.

Chapter Eight
Children's Literature
for the Primary Grade Years

Michael Searson

Literature for primary school children (roughly six to eight years old) can reflect the transition of children from a period when the world of imagination often governs their thinking and behavior to one where children have an acute awareness of the real world and the people in it as they actually exist. Children at this age are as engaged by the natural universe as they are by a world of fantasy. They have an increasingly deep and accurate knowledge about events and actions of the world, are developing good friendships (almost always with those of the same gender), can empathize with others, will likely spend as much time out of their home as in it during their waking hours, and now have internal moral mechanisms that allow them to distinguish between right and wrong. Good children's literature for this age group will embody this new awareness of the primary school child.

For many children this is a relatively stable period in which changes in their physical development are steady, but psychologically they maintain an even keel. In fact, Freud referred to the school-age years (about six to twelve) as a period of latency, in which the tension that characterizes other periods of development is not apparent. For Erikson, children at this age are attempting to demonstrate competence, at school, in sports, with friends. Piaget has characterized this period (which he refers to as "object permanence") as a time when children are grasping the complexities of the world itself and the objects within it. Lawrence Kohlberg believes that children of this age are capable of understanding and following the rules of society, including the home and the classroom. At this point, children are also concerned with behaving in ways that please others.

Although relationships with friends increase and become more stable, the school-age child will at times test relationships with family and friends. Feelings of aggression, independence, insecurity, and loneliness, among others, are likely to surface at some point or another. Books that explore these feelings and struggles should become part of children's reading experiences. The often strained relationship between George and Martha is a consistent theme throughout J. Marshall's George and Martha series (e.g., *George and Martha* [1972], *George and Martha Tons of Fun* [1972], or *George and Martha One Fine Day* [1978]). (They always end up as friends by story's end, however.) In *Mufaro's Beautiful Daughter* (Steptoe 1987), we witness a child who confronts both kindness and meanness. And we have the mischievous young mouse in *Noisy Nora* (Wells 1973) who wonders how much attention she'll get from her family when things are quiet and her disruptive behavior is no longer present. Of course, books that illuminate the positive side of relationships, such as using cooperation to ward off a foe in *Swimmy* (Lionni 1963), should also be made available. Or we can dream of beautiful and magical things, as in *Tar Beach* (Ringgold 1991). Books can also be used to offer reassurance that your family truly would be sad if you were missing, and would do everything in their power to find you, such as is the case in *Sylvester and the Magic Pebble* (Steig 1969).

Yet, for children now moving into the school years, there is the realization that the world is not simply divided into good and evil; rather, there are many times when a situation is not clearly right or wrong. Sometimes we may not make the best or correct decision; yet, this does not necessarily make us bad people. In *Two Bad Ants* (Van Allsburg 1988), the issue of initially making a flawed (and somewhat selfish) decision is rectified when the consequences of the ants' decision allow them to make amends and do what they should have done in the first place. We also have the two girls in *The Hating Book* (Zolotow 1969), who bicker throughout but who do become friends in the end because they're not quite sure what it was that they were fighting about in the first place. And then there are the truly scary and frightening thoughts that linger in the minds of all children. As I am given new responsibilities, can I truly mess things up? If I had to, could I protect my family? In *Outside Over There* (Sendak 1981), a young girl does initially drop her guard, and her baby sister is captured by goblins. In the ultimate fantasy of any young child, Ida eventually rescues her sister, fulfilling her responsibility to an absent father, and, in turn, becomes a hero. And then there is the steadfast heroine in *Brave Irene* (Steig 1986), who perseveres through all obstacles that she confronts. Most psychologists would agree that good literature serves to illuminate and allow reflection upon the inner feelings and thoughts that already exist in the innermost recesses of children's minds. (Sometimes, of course, these thoughts are more readily apparent.)

Children at this age are increasingly taking on the perspective of others and recognizing that other people have very different views and experiences even under similar circumstances (Selman 1981). After all, if you'd only let the wolf tell his side of the story about what happened to the three little pigs, as in *The True Story of the Three Little Pigs* (Scieszka 1989), you'd see that the wolf may not really be a villain. Going beyond simply taking on the perspective of others is true empathy. As you read books like *The Giving Tree* (Silverstein 1964) or *Crow Boy* (Yashima 1955) to young, school-age children, you can ask questions like, How do you think the tree feels? or How would you treat Crow Boy? Or perhaps we can imagine what Leo feels like in *Leo the Late Bloomer* (Kraus 1971); after all, there are times that we all feel incompetent at some task.

As children move (in Piaget's cognitive model) from the preoperational stage, where they perceive events in the world primarily from their own perspective and are governed by animalistic and intuitive thinking, to concrete operations, where understanding of the concrete world is established, they are enthralled by the mysteries of both the imaginative and the real worlds. Unlike the preschool child, young, school-age children do know the difference between real and make-believe. Thus fantasy of the lighter and more innocent nature is appropriate for children of this age, as they have developed metacognitive skills that make them aware of their fantasies. Yet, it is still fun to play around, and books are an important source for this fanciful enjoyment: see *Old MacDonald Had an Apartment House* by Judi Barrett (1969) and Chris Van Allsburg's *Jumanji* (1981). Of course, the classic fairy tales, such as *Rumpelstiltskin* and *Little Red Riding Hood*, continue to be enjoyed by primary grade children. Today many contemporary illustrators and authors have taken it upon themselves to rework some of these classics, see *Puss in Boots*

(1990) by Charles Perrault, illustrated by Fred Marcellino 1990; *Lon Po Po: A Red-Riding Hood Story from China*, translated and illustrated by Ed Young, 1989; *Goldilocks and the Three Bears*, retold and illustrated by James Marshall, 1988; or *The Bremen Town Musicians*, retold and illustrated by Ilse Plume, 1980, among others. The metacognitive abilities of children of this age allow them to appreciate books that poke fun at classic (and sometimes archaic) children's literature, such as is the case in *The Stinky Cheese and Other Fairly Stupid Tales* by Jon Scieszka and Lane Smith (1992) and *Father Gander Nursery Rhymes: The Equal Rhymes Amendment* (Gander 1985)

Children's ability to grapple with the mysteries of the natural world signal a new era in the types of books that should be presented to them during the primary grade years. Their fascination with the often mysterious features of the universe demand that six- to eight-year-old children be introduced to folktales. The allure that the sun, moon, oceans, rivers, and wind hold for young children is indeed reflected in many of the world's folktales. When peoples of various cultures sought to make sense of the powerful features of their natural surroundings, they inevitably resorted to folktales as a means of explaining these events before modern science yielded more rationalistic justifications. Thus, in the continental United States, tall tales, with stories of a giant and powerful man named Paul Bunyan, emerged to help make sense of a vast and unsettled wilderness. In Africa, the seemingly ever-present sun and open skies yielded stories about how the sun and the moon got in the sky in the first place. The powerful and deadly shark became a god in Hawaiian folktales. Although it is doubtful that primary grade children actually believe any of these folktales, their transition from a period where fantasy dominates to one where their thought processes are more rational and logical make it a wonderful time to explore the abundance of folktales that do exist. After all, it is sure fun to make believe.

With the cognitive capacity to comprehend real events, nonfiction, realistic fiction, and informational books also can be introduced to young school-age children. Biographies, encyclopedias (whether designed for children or the family), and historical books should be part of the nonfiction literary experience for children at this age. For example, children at this age are enthralled by the informational *First Book of. . .* series. This series includes books ranging from topics like airplanes (*The First Book of Airplanes,* Bendick 1976) to measurement (*The First Book of Measurement,* Epstein 1960) to dinosaurs (*The First Book of Prehistoric Animals,* Dickinson 1954). Realistic fiction, such as sports stories, like those by Matt Christopher (e.g., *Undercover Tailback,* 1992), or *A Very Young Gymnast* (Krementz 1978), or any of the other photojournalist-style books in this series by Jill Krementz, are among the favorites of this age group. Historical fiction such as *Working Cotton* (Williams 1992) or *Smoky Night* (Bunting 1994) should also be introduced to children of this age. These books, however, are likely to be preferred by the more mature children in the six- to eight-year-old range.

Increasing social interactions allow children to begin to take on the perspectives of others (Selman 1981). As social interactions occur outside the home, children begin to come in contact with others from different religious, ethnic, and racial backgrounds. Children's literature has increasingly become a rich medium exploring the worlds of those from different backgrounds. In *The Patchwork Quilt* (Flournoy 1985) children can witness the events that weave together the generations of an African-American family. Or they can sample the Hispanic tradition in the fascinating story of *Boorreguita and the Coyote: A Tale from Ayulta, Mexico* (Aardema 1991). Vietnamese children are represented in *Lee Ann: The Story of a Vietnamese Girl* (Brown 1991), as are Native Americans in *Baby Rattlesnake* (Ata 1989). This brief survey on books that celebrate diversity fails to do proper justice to the wide selection that now exists in today's children's literature. Yet, through discussions with librarians, bookstore owners, a little research, or paying heed to reviews of children's books in newspapers and magazines, those interested will soon find an array of literature that respectfully describes and illustrates many cultures. This is a far cry from just a generation ago when people from minority cultures were misrepresented at best or stereotyped at worst. Today, authors and illustrators take great pains to represent various groups with honesty and depth. Often the illustrators and authors themselves are members of the same groups that they are depicting.

Another major characteristic that distinguishes children of this age from previous periods is that they are now beginning to read. In other words, for the first time in their lives, young children can fully experience children's literature firsthand. They themselves can now read many of these wonderful stories. Although the intimacy with which children's literature was previously associated—sitting on the lap of a parent or teacher, lying in bed as Mom or Dad or brother or sister read aloud—may now be a thing of the past, there are some important benefits for the early reader. Children now have the ability to determine for themselves what it is they'd like to read. Whether it is in the school or at home, the child can now select the book that they want to read. There is much less negotiation between parent or teacher and child when it comes to selecting a book. Of course, teachers do assign reading selections to children during this period, but children can also choose their own readings, from the library, from the bookstore, or from a book club. For example, this is often the age at which children procure their first library card. This is also a time in which the ability of children to select their own reading material begins to shape their reading tastes. For instance, by time they reach third grade, millions of American children have developed a fascination for the R.L. Stine Goosebumps series (e.g., *Say Cheese and Die—Again!* 1996). How many of these children will develop a lifelong interest in mysteries or thrillers? Other good "early reader" books for young children include the Frog and Toad series by Arnold Lobel (e.g., *Frog and Toad Together,* 1970) or Else H. Minarik's *Little Bear* (1957) and the series that followed it. Of course, they were not written for this purpose, but children's favorite "early readers" do include the bizarre and fanciful Dr. Seuss books, such as *The Cat in the Hat* (1957), *Horton Hatches the Egg* (1940), or *And to Think That I Saw It on Mulberry Street* (1937).

Besides the empowerment that children by now have achieved by reading to themselves, the reading process is also furthered simply by reading (Turner and Paris 1995). In other words, you become a better reader by reading! So at this age, children have gained autonomy in selecting the reading material that interests them, and they now can the hone skill of reading. School reading programs that recognize the self-perpetuating nature of reading have developed activities such as "Drop Everything and Read" (DEAR), where children, along with the teacher, choose materials that interest them and read silently for enjoyment. As discussed in the previous chapter, the act of reading promotes learning and improvement in reading. Such a program would complement whatever reading approach was otherwise being taught to the children. One point to keep in mind here is that in programs such as these, or when reading at home, children should be given the opportunity to read their favorite materials (even comic books are acceptable). Remember, it is the act of reading that enhances reading, not what children read. Of course, we would hope that as they grow they would begin to read good literature, but the primary goal is to teach young children to be good readers.

The advanced intellectual level of children in the primary grades allows them to experience books that are more complex. Whether they are reading to themselves or reading aloud, children at this age can now read chapter books because they possess increased memory and attention span. Their developing cognition allows them to appreciate the elaborate language and story structures in such books. Children at this age can now experience a book over a sustained period, either by reading it themselves or by having it read to them, which may help foster lifelong good-reading habits. Children may now spend many exciting days or evenings with a pleasant spider and rambunctious pig in *Charlotte's Web* (White 1952) or they may get to know James and his strange insect friends in *James and the Giant Peach* (Dahl 1961), as they develop rich relationships with their favorite characters.

Furthermore, when children become proficient readers, they can begin to read aloud to others. Whether this happens informally (e.g., an older brother reads a story to his younger sister) or formally (e.g., in a language arts program), proficient second- or third-grade readers can read stories to younger children and attempt to make the experience enjoyable for all involved. The reader should choose a book with which he or she is comfortable. Also, an adult should be present, for management purposes, if the reader is reading to a group of young children. In addition to the enhanced language skills presented to both the reader and the listener, both groups of children can further their social skills. The reader, in fact, has now come full circle. Just a year or so earlier he or she was read to by an older person. This same reader is now sharing his or her skills in a similar context with a younger listener.

Because they are reading at a much more sophisticated level than just a few years earlier, primary grade children can now be exposed to literature that taps into this greater sophistication. Their linguistic capability has increased markedly, and their vocabulary, which is likely to be around 6,000 words by the time they're six years old, can now be challenged further. For example they may not be sure what timothy compote is in *Sylvester and the Magic Pebble* (Steig 1969), but the context clues indicate that it is probably something to eat. Further, they are using and understanding increasingly complex grammar, with conditional sentences and many conjunctives. Thus their literary experiences should match this increasingly sophisticated language structure. Thought-provoking and linguistically complex stories, such as *The Garden of Abdul Gasazi* (1979) and *Jumanji* (1981) by Chris Van Allsburg, are important to introduce to the six- to eight-year-old child. Other areas of symbolic representation have also increased in sophistication. For example, typical six- to eight-year-old children have had several years of dramatic play under their belts. They are thus delighted by stories such as *Really Rosie, Starring the Nutshell Kids* (Sendak 1975) and *Curious George Goes to the Hospital* (Rey and Rey 1966) because they include dramatic play as a focal point.

Parents and educators must realize that the primary grade years are critical in the development of a person's reading skills and habits. Therefore, the practice of reading aloud to preschool children should not be abandoned when children reach first grade and beyond. Even with increased use of electronic media, these primary grade years remain crucial to the development of appropriate lifelong reading habits; parents and teachers must continue to read aloud to primary grade children on a regular basis, while also encouraging them to read on their own.

References

Aardema, V. *Boorreguita and the Coyote: A Tale from Ayulta, Mexico*. Illustrated by Petra Mathers. New York: Knopf, 1991.

Ata, T. *Baby Rattlesnake*. Illustrated by V. Reisberg. Chicago: Children's Books Press, 1989.

Barrett, J. *Old MacDonald Had an Apartment House*. Illustrated by Ronald Barrett. New York: Atheneum, 1969.

Bendick, J. *The First Book of Airplanes*. New York: Watts, 1976.

Brown, T. *Lee Ann: The Story of a Vietnamese Girl*. New York: Putnam, 1991.

Bunting, A.E. *Smoky Night*. San Diego: Harcourt Brace Jovanovich, 1994.

Christopher, M. *Undercover Tailback*. New York: Scholastic, 1992.

Dahl, R. *James and the Giant Peach*. Illustrated by Nancy Ekholm Burkert. New York: Knopf, 1961.

Dickinson, A. *The First Book of Prehistoric Animals.* Pictures by Helene Carter. New York: Watts, 1954.

Dr. Seuss. *And to Think That I Saw It on Mulberry Street.* New York: Vanguard, 1937.

Dr. Seuss. *The Cat in the Hat.* New York: Random House, 1957.

Dr. Seuss. *Horton Hatches the Egg.* New York: Random House, 1940.

Epstein, S. *The First Book of Measurement.* New York: Watts, 1960.

Flournoy, V. *The Patchwork Quilt.* Illustrated by J. Pinkney. New York: Dial, 1985.

Gander, F. *Father Gander Nursery Rhymes: The Equal Rhymes Amendment.* Illustrated by Carolyn. Santa Barbara, Calif.: Advocacy Press, 1985.

Kraus, R. *Leo the Late Bloomer.* Illustrated by Jose Aruego. New York: Windmill, 1971.

Krementz, J. *A Very Young Gymnast.* New York: Knopf, 1978.

Leaf, M. *The Story of Ferdinand.* Illustrated by Robert Lawson. New York: Viking, 1936.

Lionni, L. *Swimmy.* New York: Pantheon, 1963.

Lobel, A. *Frog and Toad Together.* New York: Harper & Row, 1970.

Marshall, J. *George and Martha.* Boston: Houghton Mifflin, 1972.

Marshall, J. *George and Martha One Fine Day.* Boston: Houghton Mifflin, 1978.

Marshall, J. *George and Martha Tons of Fun.* Boston: Houghton Mifflin, 1972.

Marshall, J. *Goldilocks and the Three Bears.* New York: Dial, 1988.

Minarik, E.H. *Little Bear.* Illustrated by Maurice Sendak. New York: Harper & Row, 1957.

Perrault, C. *Puss in Boots.* Illustrated by Fred Marcellino. New York: Farrar Straus and Giroux, 1990.

Plume, I. *The Bremen Town Musicians.* New York: Doubleday, 1980.

Rey, M. and H.A. Rey. *Curious George Goes to the Hospital.* Boston: Houghton Mifflin, 1966.

Ringgold, F. *Tar Beach.* New York: Crown, 1991.

Scieszka, J. *The Stinky Cheese Man and Other Fairly Stupid Tales.* Illustrated by Lane Smith. New York: Viking, 1992.

Scieszka, J. *The True Story of the Three Little Pigs.* Illustrated by Lane Smith. New York: Viking, 1989.

Selman, R.L. "The Child As a Friendship Philosopher." In S. Ascher and J. Gottman (eds.), *The Development of Children's Friendships.* Cambridge, Eng.: Cambridge University Press, 1981.

Sendak, M. *Outside Over There.* New York: Harper & Row, 1981.

Sendak, M. *Really Rosie, Starring the Nutshell Kids.* New York: Harper & Row, 1975.

Silverstein, S. *The Giving Tree.* New York: Harper & Row, 1964.

Steig, W. *Brave Irene.* New York: Farrar Straus and Giroux, 1986.

Steig, W. *Sylvester and the Magic Pebble.* New York: Simon & Schuster, 1969.

Steptoe, J. *Mufaro's Beautiful Daughter.* New York: Lothrop, Lee and Shepard, 1987.

Stine, R.L. *Say Cheese and Die—Again!* New York: Scholastic, 1996.

Turner, J. and S.G. Paris. "How Literacy Tasks Influence Children's Motivation for Literacy." *The Reading Teacher, 48,* 1995, pp. 662–673.

Van Allsburg, C. *The Garden of Abdul Gasazi.* Boston: Houghton Mifflin, 1979.

Van Allsburg, C. *Jumanji.* Boston: Houghton Mifflin, 1981.

Van Allsburg, C. *Two Bad Ants.* Boston: Houghton Mifflin, 1988.

Wells, R. *Noisy Nora.* New York: Dial, 1973.

White, E.B. *Charlotte's Web.* Illustrated by Garth Williams. New York: Harper & Row, 1952.

Williams, S.A. *Working Cotton.* Illustrated by C. Byard. San Diego: Harcourt Brace Jovanovich, 1992.

Yashima, T. *Crow Boy.* New York: Viking, 1955.

Young, E. *Lon Po Po: A Red-Riding Hood Story from China.* New York: Philomel Books, 1989.

Zolotow, C. *The Hating Book.* Illustrated by Ben Shecter. New York: Harper & Row, 1969.

Chapter Nine
The Making of Children's Videos Based on Picture Books
The Weston Woods Story

Cari Best

Morton Schindel, founder of Weston Woods Studios, was a pioneering spirit and a spirited artist. In 1953, he decided to respond to people's complaints that there was nothing good on television for children. He wanted to find out what would be regarded as "something good" and see if he could fill that need.

Schindel became familiar with some of the outstanding picture books of that time—*Make Way for Ducklings, Madeline, Little Toot,* and *Millions of Cats*—but he was not entusiastic about the prospect of translating sensitive line drawings to the film medium. It took him fourteen months to complete his first film. When he started, he put an illustration on the wall and moved the camera on it, but the far side of the picture appeared bigger than the near side. He then decided to keep the camera steady and create a moving easel. That worked. The pictures themselves suggested the camera's speed and the direction of movement. Schindel came to call his method "iconography," and it was used when a book could not be animated with fidelity to the original using standard techniques.

Today other film companies (e.g., Rabbit Ears Productions) and television programs (e.g., Reading Rainbow and Storytime) have embraced Schindel's innovative technique. Ernest Boyer, who headed the Carnegie Foundation's Ready to Learn research project in the early 1990s, continues to forward Schindel's tradition of excellence. In his book *Ready to Learn: A Mandate for the Nation* (1992), Boyer maintains that next to a parent, television is a child's most influential teacher. Whether it's a six-month-old peering between the rails of her crib or a three-year-old excitedly awaiting his favorite noontime show or a kindergartner who is able to manipulate the remote control buttons as well as any adult, the amount of time young children spend watching television is astounding. If nineteen million preschoolers are said to watch about two hours a day, then altogether in one year, they would watch roughly fourteen billion hours!

While television has the potential, like all good teachers, to ignite curiosity and introduce new worlds to children (and in many cases it does), children for the most part are being bombarded with random offerings of irrelevant commercials, violent situations, and lightning-fast images that tend to shorten their attention spans, affect their powers of concentration, and hamper their language development.

Peggy Charren, a staunch advocate for children's rights and founder of Action for Children's Television, contends that "too many people in the television business are figuring out how to benefit from children instead of how to benefit children."

Ernest Boyer advises that in order for the best of television to contribute significantly to school readiness, parents must take an active role in their children's viewing habits, just as they influence decisions about sleeping and eating.

Charren, also a highly effective voice for parental involvement, agrees that parents and other caregivers need to know about the good television programs and children's videos in order to target them for their children.

The advantage of video over television is that parents can determine exactly when and what their children will be watching. For parents of young children, it is this single outstanding factor—the degree of control and free choice that the videocassette recorder allows them to exercise—that makes this machine such a godsend. Concerned parents and caregivers can then be their own television programmers, broadcasting only those shows that they want their children to see. No longer is children's programming entirely in the hands of television executives and corporate sponsors, whose main concern has sometimes been, regrettably, to take advantage of the rapt audience of young children, fascinated by anything moving on the small screen.

The VCR, when used in the very best way—with well-selected videos—can nurture a child's mind and imagination and provide physical exercise. A VCR can showcase timeless stories that help with word use and vocabulary, teach ways in which to share and be sociable, and introduce a child to fine art and music. But most importantly, a good video will delight a child in every sense of the word, and will continue to provide meaningful pleasure even after repeated viewings.

It cannot be emphasized enough at this point how important it is for adults to prescreen every video that children will watch, and without exception, look at the images on the screen through the eyes of a child. Parents, teachers, and other caregivers who know their children better than anyone will, of course, act in their best interests.

Because children at a young age tend to be easily startled or frightened or disturbed, and one child's tickled funny bone might be another child's recurring nightmare, it is infinitely better to err on the safe side.

The following is a useful set of guidelines that all children's video prescreeners should follow:

- What is the appropriate age range for kids watching the video?
- Does the video contain anything that might frighten or disturb a young child?
- Does the video contain any violence or aggression? If so, how is it handled?
- Does the video present gender, ethnic, or cultural stereotyping?
- How are the video's production values (sound, animation, photography, etc.)?
- Does the video inspire children's imaginations, learning, and/or play?
- Is this a video to buy or to rent? How often can a child watch the tape and still find it interesting?

So how do we go about deciding which are the best videos produced for children? In his introductory guide to selecting outstanding children's videos, Scott Blakey, critic and columnist for the *Los Angeles Times,* suggests that the so-called best ones will honor "the magic of childhood," without condescending or preaching, and leave enough room for the child to learn and to grow (1995).

"The finest children's videos offer the same rewards as good children's literature—satisfying, emotionally meaningful stories presented in a rich, imaginative style," writes Dr. Harold Schechter, editorial adviser for the *Journal of Popular Culture* in the 1980s, in one of the first parents' guides to children's videos: *Kidvid* (1986).

Likewise, the American Library Association maintains that some of the best children's books have been transformed into videos, giving children the chance to gain "video literacy" by observing a range of production techniques from live action to animation to iconography. Children learn how to watch, assess, and interpret—to think while looking—and, most of all, how to make connections with other experiences, including reading. They learn about art, narration, and music from watching a skillfully produced video. Just think of the power of that small screen to influence the way children think!

Videos are not meant to be substitutes for quality time with a parent or for good books. Neither are the good children's videos time wasters or appetite spoilers when it comes time to read, although many parents do worry that watching video stories may kill their children's interest in books. One group's experience underscores the fact that good books on video can, in fact, have the opposite effect, whetting kids' appetites for reading and being read to.

This was found to be the case when a group of researchers gathering information for an upcoming *Sesame Street Parents' Guide* got together and exposed their "kid testers" to a variety of book-based tapes. After the screening was completed, the group, composed of kids and adults, chose only those videos they considered outstanding for the "consistent quality of the story adaptations." Along with several single video titles, one entire series was recommended without reservation. That series was the Children's Circle Library, established in 1984 as the home video division of Weston Woods. Weston Woods has been the principal innovator in the translation of picture books into the audiovisual media and a pioneer in the multimedia approach to children's literature since 1953.

What is remarkable about Weston Woods/Children's Circle, and its founder, Morton Schindel, is that when he began to produce films in the mid-1950s, there was virtually no market for the kinds of movies he wanted to make—small, serious films that would attempt to re-create and thus preserve the expressive quality of the original picture books upon which they were based. John Cech, in *Weston Woods: Three Decades of Moving Picture Books* (1989), calls these films "acts of celebration" of love for an artistic form that had grown out of Schindel's own experience reading to his children and, in the process, being moved to make the production of these films his life's work.

Though he calls himself an "edutainer," Schindel has wanted his films to serve as a means of drawing children back to books, sending them off excitedly to the library, not to toy stores or to theme parks.

It is our role at Weston Woods to create audiovisual adaptations that are faithful reflections of the books themselves. We seek the best books from all over the world and adapt them in such a way as to preserve the integrity of the original. By so doing, we help children discover the riches that are trapped between the covers of books and motivate them to want to read for themselves. We believe that a child who wants to read will easily learn to read, and we believe that a child without reading problems will be a child without learning problems. (Weston Woods, preface)

From the earliest iconographic adaptations of such works as James Daugherty's *Andy and the Lion* and Virginia Lee Burton's *Mike Mulligan and His Steam Shovel* to the fully animated versions of Rosemary Wells's *Morris's Disappearing Bag* or Maurice Sendak's *In the Night Kitchen*, Weston Woods intended to take the road not taken by commercial studios.

Before Weston Woods was established, a few attempts had been made to base films on picture books. Walt Disney had produced film versions of *The Little House* by Virginia Lee Burton, *Ferdinand the Bull* by Robert Lawson, and *Little Toot* by Hardie Gramatky. These films were designed to precede the main feature in commercial movie theaters, and the stories were therefore rewritten to appeal to diversified audiences. The original book illustrations were not used in the films; they were supplanted by pictures drawn in the graphic style of the Disney Studios.

The first effort to transpose a children's picture book to the screen with fidelity to the original came in 1952, when United Productions of America adapted Ludwig Bemelman's *Madeline*. The film was an artistic success, but the market for theatrical shorts did not last. It gave way to longer features, so no sustained production resulted from this initial effort.

Meanwhile, Schindel moved ahead with his plan to make motion pictures that remained faithful to the original book. He decided to bypass commercial theaters and offer the programs where children would have an opportunity to see them: in schools and libraries, and on television. He followed a course no other film producer had taken:

I consulted with specialists in the children's book field, combed the library shelves, talked with authors and illustrators and came up with a list of time-tested books with universal appeal.

I knew that for the films to be successful, each adaptation must retain the artist's intent and, as much as possible, be a "mirror image" of the book. I felt it was my responsibility to the authors and illustrators to present their work on screen just as it appeared in their books. (Weston Woods, 3)

This concept of "fidelity to the original" became the philosophical underpinning of Weston Woods. Picture books that meet the rigorous standards set by Weston Woods are adapted in a variety of media using a multitude of production techniques suited to the nature of the story and its graphic style. Schindel's iconographic technique has been used successfully by Weston Woods and by other film producers as well.

Unlike animation, where hundreds of pictures are hand-drawn to create motion, in Schindel's iconographic photography the entire static illustration moves in front of a stationary camera. Hovering over the book illustrations, much as a child would examine them, the camera probes for the elements that contribute to the total composition of each picture. By emphasizing one detail and then another as it corresponds to the text, and by moving in deliberate directions at controlled speeds, the camera captures the mood and action that the illustrator implied on the pages of the book.

Schindel found that this technique could complement the book by helping viewers see familiar things in new ways and discover details they may not have noticed before. "Iconographic" soon became a familiar word in the filmmaker's vocabulary.

The success of films based on picture books gave rise to a demand for comparable films for older children. This prompted the Weston Woods staff to seek the best books for young readers. The short stories in *Homer Price* by Robert McCloskey seemed ideal for adaptation as live-action films. In 1964, Weston Woods produced McCloskey's *The Doughnuts,* the first short live-action dramatic film based on a children's book ever to be produced in the United States. These live-action films of stories that have few illustrations but use words to describe the characters, action, and mood of the story.

With the introduction of live-action films based on children's books, Weston Woods once again broke new ground in the storytelling tradition. In a 1989 *Horn Book* article John Cech compares Weston Woods to the Disney Studios. He notes that in the early 1960s Weston Woods got its big break when the first dozen Weston Woods films began their long run on the television show *Captain Kangaroo.* Schindel allowed them to be shown without a Weston Woods credit line—a gesture that would have been inconceivable for Disney, with whom Schindel is most often compared.

Both Disney and Schindel adapted children's books to film. However, Schindel was interested in preserving the unique quality of the book's language and art, and thus its integrity as a whole, as compared to Walt Disney's reworkings of the classics and less familiar books. Disney felt no compunction about radically changing the nature of the originals when it suited his purposes; and, while his instincts for fashioning works that could entertain served him well in his film of *Pinocchio,* these same drives turned other works that depended on the subtleties of their literary and artistic styles—like *Winnie the Pooh* and *Peter Pan*—into echoes of the real thing. Schindel's works remained true to the stories, reflecting the author's intentions.

In the *Modern Language Association Division on Children's Literature Annual,* published in 1981, Schindel shared his dream in which picture books and movies would together preserve the objectives and uphold the standards of great literature for children, the components of each directed toward the ultimate goal of stimulating and developing the imagination:

In my dream I even see youngsters turning from the screen toward adults, beseeching them to "read to me"—and adults turning to youngsters and saying, "Let me read to you." In this way, televised stories may serve as my films have always been designed to do: revive the imagination of both child and adult and bring them together in a shared voyage of discovery.

In the words of John Cech at the close of his 1989 *Horn Book* article, he expressed hope that Weston Woods would continue to "stick to its knitting"—to produce "more of those sparkling gems that have dazzled children back to books, helping them to see and hear and feel" the riches that are waiting to be discovered in books. These children's stories when communicated through the medium of videos can be every bit as imaginative and artful as the stories that are told in print.

A sample selection from the Children's Circle Home Video Library family viewing is included in Chapter eleven, "A Reading and Resources List."

References

Blakey, Scott. *Kidvid: How to Select Kids' Videos for Your Family*. New York: HarperCollins, 1995.

Boyer, Ernest. *Ready to Learn: A Mandate for the Nation*. Lawrenceville, N.J.: Carnegie Foundation for the Advancement of Teaching, 1992.

Cech, John. "Weston Woods: Three Decades of Moving Picture Books," *The Horn Book*, Sept./Oct. 1989, pp. 589–594.

Copple, Carol and Robin Morris. "Classics on the Screen," *Sesame Street Parents' Guide*, Oct. 1993, p. 23.

Schechter, Harold. *Kidvid: A Parents' Guide to Children's Videos*. New York: Simon & Schuster, 1986.

Schindel, Morton. "Children's Literature on Film: Through the Audiovisual Era to the Age of Telecommunications," *Annual of the Modern Language Association, Division on Children's Literature and the Children's Literature Association*. New Haven: Yale University Press, 1981.

Weston Woods. *Storytelling in the Audiovisual Media*. Weston, CT: Weston Woods, 1986.

Chapter Ten
Interactive Children's Literature for Early Childhood

Christine Baykowski
Nicole R. Vogel
Michael Searson

A generation ago a small, innovative company, Weston Woods, used the dominant communications technology of the day to offer young children a novel way to experience their favorite stories. (See Chapter Nine for more details about this venture.) Today a similar transformation in the way that children encounter literature is taking place. The technology used by Weston Woods that allowed children to explore literature was film and video. Many classic children's literature titles, including Caldecott Award winners, were transferred to film and video, using the original illustrations of the book and an appealing voice that read unaltered text. Children were able to complement their book experience with one that reflected modern technology, the use of video and film. Likewise, today many children's classics are being transformed into interactive computer software. As with the Weston Woods enterprise, the intent is for modern technology to complement rather than replace actual books.

In this chapter we will discuss interactive children's literature, sometimes referred to as talking books or interactive storybooks. We will list and describe in detail the evaluation criteria that we use to select quality interactive children's literature for classrooms. Methods that teachers can use to incorporate these CD-ROM storybooks into daily classroom instruction will also be discussed. Our review will conclude with a look toward the future on how the Internet may be used in early childhood classrooms, and, finally, an annotated selection of quality interactive children's literature is provided.

A major objective of an early childhood program is the development and acquisition of reading skills. How best to teach these skills is an issue that early childhood educators have struggled with for years. According to the guidelines for appropriate curriculum content and assessment set by the National Association for the Education of Young Children (1990), teachers need to provide an environment that consists of stimulating experiences and activities. When it comes to the development of reading skills, research has shown that young children can become competent readers when they are immersed in a print-rich, literate environment and are involved in daily literature experiences (Zucker 1993).

Educators have recognized the importance of integrating technology into everyday learning (Truett 1993). Today, when delivering the richest software with abundant graphic and audio support, the CD-ROM is the format of choice. And when it comes to the educational software, CD-ROM technology is being incorporated into many early childhood classrooms (McCarthy 1993). In particular, storybooks on CD-ROMs are increasingly used as part of the reading and language arts curricula (DeJean, Miller, and Olson 1995).

In this review we will highlight those books that we consider to be classics. Good literature always has been an integral part of the early childhood classroom, because educators realize that when children are read to they develop fluency in oral language (Hornburger 1994). Additionally, involvement in daily literature experiences also contributes to critical thinking skills, decision-making skills, and other forms of learning. Some books become favorites of parents, children, and educators because of their beautiful illustrations and entertaining story lines. Over time, these stories by well-known authors become known as classics, by children, parents, and educators. Many of these classic stories are now available as interactive children's literature, on CD-ROMs, such as *Tales of Benjamin Bunny* (1991) by Beatrix Potter, *Green Eggs and Ham* (1996) by Dr. Seuss, and *Just Me and My Dad* (1994) by Mercer Mayer.

There are now hundreds of language arts educational software titles. Many of these rely on children's stories. Yet, there are those that do not offer interactive features. They simply turn the pages, and the student remains a passive listener. We will specifically focus on interactive classic children's literature, which is usually presented in multimedia form on CD-ROM. Interactive storybooks like these allow children to be active participants in their learning. This supports the theories on how children learn by constructivist theorists like Piaget and Vygotsky, who argue that knowledge is not taught. Rather, they contend, children actively construct knowledge through self-initiated manipulation (NAEYC 1990). Interactive storybooks encourage this kind of manipulation by placing control in the hands of learners and allowing them to become decision makers.

In some cases, the software emphasizes the development of language and vocabulary. For example, Discis Books, one type of interactive storybook, empowers children by encouraging independent reading. Children no longer need to be frustrated by an unfamiliar word or sentence. They can manipulate the program to pronounce individual words in syllables, supply definitions, and offer sample sentences for unknown words (Balajthy 1994).

In other cases, the software is interactive, but does not utilize classic children's literature. Whereas, some interactive programs may include children's stories, the software publisher may have chosen to use titles other than classics. In the Scholastics' *Wiggle Works* series, for example, the programs utilize outstanding graphics for the children to view and many innovative interactive features. This series, however, relies on stories that were created by the publisher for the enhancement of beginning readers' literacy skills. *Wiggle Works* uses stories that have been developed to build children's reading skills in an incremental fashion. The entire series, in fact, progresses in increasingly complex levels of sophistication. In the end, however, the stories, as a group, cannot be considered classic children's literature.

The best examples of interactive children's literature utilize CD-ROM technology, which affords the software publisher the ability to incorporate sophisticated audio, graphics, and a user-friendly environment into the program (Searson 1994). CD-ROM storybooks can offer sophisticated graphics that are similar or exact copies of the original storybook version (DeJean, Miller, and Olson 1995). To truly appreciate the beauty of the graphics, a color monitor is essential. In Living Books the children have the option of clicking on the pictures to make them move in amusing ways. For example, in the multimedia version of *Aesop's Fables: The Tortoise and the Hare* (1994), the user clicks on the starting flag and watches as the duck family waddles over to wish the tortoise and the hare good luck. And by clicking on the muskrat, the user can listen as the character strums his banjo. Another unique feature is the variety of ways that text is used. The text can be read by the children at their own pace. As the story is read by the computer, the sentences are highlighted so that they can be easily followed by the children. Discis Books offer the option of customizing the text. The font, size, style, and line spacing of the words can be altered by clicking on the text. Finally, when a picture is clicked, its name appears and the label is read aloud.

Talking books are able to offer realistic sound because of the large storage capacity of CDs (Simonson and Simonson 1997). Realistic sound and high-quality graphics are two features that make CD-ROM talking books valuable additions to any classroom library. With this advanced technology, books can be read expressively to the children in a human voice, which, according to Truett (1993), adds meaning to the story. The children are able to grasp the meaning of the story because when stories are read with expression, children become familiar with the feelings of the characters. For example, in the Living Books version of *The Berenstain Bears Get Stage Fright* (1995) by Stan and Jan Berenstain, children can hear the anger in Brother Bear's voice as the text is read. Understanding the character's feelings helps children comprehend what is taking place.

Music and sound graphics are two additional components that enhance the telling of the story. In the Living Books version of *Arthur's Birthday* (1994) by Marc Brown there is a seemingly never-ending number of fascinating pictures to explore. By clicking on the teapot the user can watch the steam rise as the teapot whistles and dances to the music. By clicking on the calendar, the user can watch the blinking lights announce the date of Arthur's birthday. Music accompanies the main characters as they introduce each Living Book, so that the user can, for example, dance along with Brother and Sister Berenstain Bear as they welcome the user to Bear Country.

The opportunity to offer translations of stories into other languages can be a vital feature in many classrooms. An NAEYC 1990 position statement addresses the importance of recognizing cultural differences and language diversity among students. Many interactive storybooks are available in Spanish, French, Japanese, and even Cantonese. CD-ROM storybooks can serve as valuable teaching tools for work with bilingual students. They also may provide students with the opportunity to share their native language with others. Living Books and Discis Books translate the stories into a variety of languages, which can ease the transition into the classroom for a child who is a non-English-speaking student. With a push of a key the text and narration can be changed from English to any of the other languages offered. Books by well-known authors such as Mercer Mayer, Marc Brown, Beatrix Potter, and Dr. Seuss can be enjoyed in various languages.

When choosing CD-ROM storybooks for the classroom, there are certain evaluation criteria that should be considered. We suggest the following as major criteria to guide the selection of quality interactive children's literature: first, the programs *must* be truly interactive. Second, although many interactive programs are available, we recommend those that rely on children's classics. Finally, we recommend those programs that best facilitate integration into the language arts curriculum.

An early childhood educator must be certain that the program is interactive. There are electronic storybooks that merely "turn the pages" for the students but do not offer any specialized features. The child can listen as the story is read but cannot interact in any way. Yet, in an early childhood setting, learning should be as interactive as possible. The NAEYC 1990 position statement has taken the position that children need to participate actively in the learning process. They should not be passive listeners, but must be able to engage in activities that are meaningful to them. For example, an interactive feature in the Living Books series is the option for the child to click on pictures and characters to make them move and talk. In this way, the literary experience becomes multidimensional.

The selection of quality interactive children's literature should begin with classics, by popular children's authors, such as Mercer Mayer, Dr. Seuss, and Beatrix Potter. These standards have been enjoyed by children for years. Now children can experience their old favorites in new and exciting ways. In addition to a good story, the best of interactive children's literature should include colorful replicas of the original storybook version. Children have become accustomed to characters looking a certain way. Well-known characters should be portrayed in the same manner whether it be in book form, on a video, or on a computer screen.

When choosing CD-ROM storybooks it is beneficial to select those that are accompanied by teacher support materials, which make integrating this type of software into the classroom even more effective. It allows educators to combine their ideas with a variety of different extensions. These support materials may include teacher guides, reproducibles, or even concrete materials that may be used alongside the software to enhance the experience and, perhaps, provide evaluation of student progress.

Whether the program actually includes support materials, teachers can find innovative ways to incorporate interactive children's literature into their language arts program. In one classroom, CD-ROM storybooks were integrated into the curriculum through an "Author of the Month" program. An extension of the reading program, it included a study of the author's life and at least one story by the highlighted author read aloud each day by the teacher. In addition, art and creative writing activities that related to the individual stories were planned. Studying an author's life makes children realize that real people write stories. It allows them to visualize that they can become authors one day. This motivates them to begin to write creative stories on their own. Children love to see themselves as authors whose stories are read by others. Four of the authors studied were Marc Brown, Mercer Mayer, and Stan and Jan Berenstain. The students had enjoyed stories by these well-known authors for many years. And some of these stories normally included in the "Author of the Month" program are now available in multimedia form, through CD-ROM technology. Titles include *Just Me and My Dad* (1994) and *Little Monster at School* by Mercer Mayer (1994), *Arthur's Birthday* (1994) and *Arthur's Teacher Trouble* (1994) by Marc Brown, and *Berenstain Bears Get Stage Fright* by Stan and Jan Berenstain (1995). These interactive talking books allow children to experience classic children's literature complemented by the advances of technology.

Interactive storybooks can also either be incorporated into a whole language approach or be used to reinforce skills with which children may be having difficulty. In the Living Books series, teacher guides are available for each CD-ROM storybook. The guides describe ways that these storybooks can be integrated into the curriculum. They also include activity plans, reproducibles, a thematic unit, annotated bibliographies, and additional teaching resources, as well as technical, practical, and curricular support. One extension activity suggested for the Living Books version of *Arthur's Teacher Trouble* by Marc Brown (1994) NYPL is to observe, record, and orally describe events that occur following the click of the mouse (Penso and Saccardi 1994). Children will choose a picture to click on and record the actions that resulted from their mouse click, and they can share their findings with their classmates.

Another extension activity the children can enjoy is started by clicking on the "Let Me Play" mode. Here the children can see a visual representation of how the story's character is feeling. If the text says, "She felt sad today," then by clicking the character, she will display a sad face. This activity encourages the students to read more carefully and consider viewpoints and perspectives other than their own. (Of course, the ability to take on the perspectives of others is a characteristic of the Piagetian stage of concrete operations, which represents most children in the primary grade years.) Children can be placed in small groups and given a character from the story to study. The computer will find all the pages that feature the assigned character. The students can find out about the character's actions in the story and reactions to the plot. This information can be recorded in student journals and later shared in a class discussion on the story.

Another activity suggested by Penso and Saccardi (1994), often one of the children's favorites, allows them to play detective. For example, in the Living Books *Arthur's Teacher Trouble* (Brown 1994), an airplane is hidden on every page. Children can be broken into groups and assigned the task of finding the airplanes. They can then write clues for other students to use. These clues can be recorded on reproducibles, which are provided along with the program and kept in a folder by the computer for easy reference.

Many of the features offered on Discis CD-ROM storybooks can be customized by the teacher to meet the special needs of specific children. One feature that can be individualized by the teacher is the speed at which the story is read. This is beneficial for slower readers. The style and size of the print can also be changed according to student preference.

Integrating technology with literature adds another dimension to children's learning experiences. According to the National Association for the Education of Young Children (1990) all children have different styles of learning. Therefore, the curriculum should incorporate a broad range of experiences and activities that meet individual needs. As stated above, CD-ROM storybooks are another way of involving children in literature experiences. Not only are they beneficial for this reason, but they offer a vast amount of text, sound, and graphical features. These features address the multitude of learning styles that children have.

There are times when a teacher is working with other students and is not immediately available to one child. Discis Books enable children to read the story without the immediate assistance of a teacher. As mentioned earlier, children can click on an unknown word to receive the pronunciation or a definition. The words that the children click on are stored on a recall list that can be retrieved by the teacher at a later date. This enables the teacher to know which words the children had difficulty with so they can be reviewed in future lessons.

As with the printed versions, interactive storybooks can be used individually or in cooperative groups. The NAEYC 1990 position statement explains that social interaction among peers is crucial for developing positive social behavior. Children can learn from one another, which helps them move to higher levels of understanding. Social interaction also helps children learn how to work and play cooperatively.

On the other hand, some electronic storybooks offer benefits for children working alone. By navigating through text by themselves students become more independent readers because they do not have to rely on the teacher to explain words or terms. With talking storybooks, the child has easy access to information such as definitions and pronunciations, simply by clicking on words or sentences. This is especially beneficial for students who are unwilling to ask for assistance. Once a word is selected by the student it is saved by the computer on a "recall list." At a later date, the teacher can refer to the recall list for a record of those words with which students had difficulty. The teacher can now incorporate these words into future vocabulary activities, and even add the words to children's vocabulary lists. Later, the teacher can look for these words to appear in student writing activities. Additionally, the children can hear the words read aloud by the computer, syllable by syllable. In this way, the children's spoken vocabulary can increase. The teacher may also have the children list these new vocabulary words on charts according to the number of syllables they contain. The children should be encouraged to share these vocabulary charts during group activities.

Computer technology often provides a neutral forum for children who feel more comfortable when a machine, rather than a teacher, assesses their work. The computer thus functions as an "adult or more capable peer" in a Vygotskian sense. Vygotsky (1962) said we cannot look at what children are capable of doing when they are working alone, but we must see how far ahead they can go when offered assistance. He refers to this as the "zone of proximal development."

Teacher attitudes toward technology determine the extent to which computers are used in the classroom (DeJean, Miller, and Olson 1995). When teachers do not feel comfortable with computers or do not believe them to be beneficial, the other computer-related technologies, such as CD-ROMs, are not utilized. Teachers need to feel confident that storybooks on CD-ROM are of value to their students. They must know how to incorporate them effectively into the existing reading and language arts curricula. Although they may feel uncomfortable with, or even resistant to, computer technology, early childhood teachers regularly use a variety of literary formats in their daily instruction, including poetry, nonfiction books, magazines, fairy tales, multicultural tales, picture books, and big books. Interactive storybooks simply add a new dimension to classrooms, exposing children to yet another literature format.

A final component to be considered when developing a library of interactive children's literature is nonfiction. The electronic versions of these rich informational books, are often even more compelling. In fact, this genre provides some of the most spectacular examples of interactive multimedia. Two of the best examples for the early childhood collection are from Dorling Kindersley Multimedia, *The Way Things Work* (Macaulay 1996) and *My First Incredible Amazing Dictionary* (Dorling Kindersley 1994). Both of these titles are filled with abundant information about a variety of topics from the common to the strange. And they are supported by rich graphics and sound. They can easily be incorporated into a variety of classroom projects and activities.

As we look toward the future we can expect to see networking and telecommunications becoming a vital part of early childhood and primary grade classrooms (Brett 1994). On-line services such as AT&T Learning Network and Kids Network are two student-oriented information services that are specifically designed for use in the classrooms. Children are no longer restricted only to what occurs in their school. Being on-line gives them the opportunity to converse and to exchange ideas with other classrooms near and far (Brett 1994). On-line services and the Internet enable students and teachers to access information and communicate with others like never before. Unfortunately, the technology required to deliver sophisticated on-line audio and graphics is not yet available in all classrooms. For the moment, the CD-ROM format is likely to remain the standard for the delivery of quality interactive children's literature.

In summary, it is essential that CD-ROM storybooks do not become substitutions to books. Teachers must continue to read to their students and share the joys of literacy. The intimacy and physical sharing apparent when real books are read aloud remains a truly special experience. Talking storybooks can be a welcome addition to an already rich classroom library but should not replace books.

Interactive Children's Literature for the Early Childhood Classroom

Nonfiction

The Way Things Work by David Macaulay
My First Incredible Amazing Dictionary by Dorling Kindersley

Dorling Kindersley Multimedia
Houghton Mifflin
95 Madison Avenue
New York, NY 10016

This multimedia series of nonfiction reference books offers children a new way of exploring science and technology concepts and the meanings of words. With a click of a mouse each word, scientific principle, and invention is explained and illustrated in amazing detail. These resource books combine fascinating animations and sounds as they lead children down an educational path of new discoveries.

Fiction

Titles from the Living Books series:

Arthur's Birthday, by Marc Brown
Arthur's Teacher Trouble, by Marc Brown
The Berenstain Bears Get Stage Fright, by Stan and Jan Berenstain
Green Eggs and Ham, by Dr. Seuss
Just Me and My Dad, by Mercer Mayer
Aesop's Fables: The Tortoise and the Hare

Living Books
Broderbund Software, Inc.
500 Redwood Blvd.
Novato, CA 94948

Living Books are multimedia versions of original storybooks written by well-known children's authors. Their beautiful illustrations and unique use of sound and music keep children engaged for hours. Clicking on pictures causes actions to occur that add detail to the stories. This program provides a wonderful way to develop reading skills. These stories can be experienced by children in English, Spanish, or Japanese. Children will truly enjoy and learn from these programs.

Titles from the Discis Books series:

Tales of Benjamin Bunny, by Beatrix Potter
Cinderella
The Tale of Peter Rabbit, by Beatrix Potter

Discis Books: Discis Knowledge Research, Inc.
NYCCPO Box #45099
Toronto, Ontario, Canada M2N 6NZ

Discis Books provide a wonderful way for children to develop word recognition, vocabulary, and reading comprehension skills. The illustrations are duplicates of the original storybook versions. Children can interact by clicking on pictures and words for definitions and pronunciations. These interactive storybooks are also provided in Spanish, French, and Cantonese.

References

Aesop's Fables: The Tortoise and the Hare. [Computer software]. Novato, Calif.: Living Books, 1994.

Balajthy, E. *Whole Language, Computers and CD-ROM Technology: A Kindergarten Unit on "Benjamin Bunny"* (ERIC Document Reproduction Service No. ED 364831), 1994.

Berenstain, S. and J. Berenstain. *The Berenstain Bears Get Stage Fright*. (Computer Software). Navato, Calif. Broderbund Software, Inc., 1995.

Brett, A. "Online for New Learning Opportunities." *Dimensions of Early Childhood, 22* (1994): 10–13.

Brown, M. *Arthur's Birthday*. [Computer software]. Novato, Calif.: Living Books, 1994.

Brown, M. *Arthur's Teacher Trouble*. [Computer software]. Novato, Calif.: Living Books, 1994.

DeJean, J., L. Miller, and J. Olson. *CD-ROM Talking Books: A Case Study of Promise and Practice*. Spencer Foundation, Chicago, Ill. (ERIC Document Reproduction Service No. ED 385217), 1995.

Dorling Kindersley. *My First Incredible Amazing Dictionary*. [Computer software]. New York: Dorling Kindersley Multimedia, 1994.

Dr. Seuss. *Green Eggs and Ham*. [Computer software]. Novato, Calif.: Living Books, 1996.

Hornburger, J. "Bringing Children and Books Together: Learning through Literature." In H. Nuba, M. Searson, and D.L. Sheiman (eds.), *Resources for Early Childhood: A Handbook*. New York: Garland, 1994, pp. 335–342.

Macaulay, D. *The Way Things Work*. [Computer software]. New York: Dorling Kindersley Multimedia, 1996.

Mayer, M. *Just Me and My Dad*. [Computer software]. Novato, Calif.: Living Books, 1994.

Mayer, M. *Little Monster at School* [Computer software]. Novato, Calif.: Living Books, 1994.

McCarthy, R. "CD-ROM Spins into Schools." *Electronic Learning, 13* (1993): 10–15.

National Association for the Education of Young Children (NAEYC). "Position Statement on Standardized Testing of Young Children 3 through 8 Years of Age." *Young Children, 43* (1990): 42–47.

Penso, R. and M. Saccardi. *Classroom Activities for Arthur's Teacher Trouble*. Novato, Calif.: Living Books, 1994.

Potter, B. *Tales of Benjamin Bunny*. [Computer software.] Buffalo, N.Y.: Discis Knowledge Research, 1991.

Potter, B. *The Tale of Peter Rabbit*. [Computer software.] Buffalo, N.Y.: Discis Knowledge Research, 1991.

Searson, M. "Computers in Early Childhood Education." In H. Nuba, M. Searson, and D. Sheiman (eds.), *Resources for Early Childhood: A Handbook*. New York: Garland, 1994, pp. 417-435..

Simonson, M.R. and A. Simonson. *Educational Computing Foundation*. Upper Saddle River, N.J.: Merrill, 1997.

Truett, C. "CD-ROM Storybooks Bring Children's Literature to Life." *The Computing Teacher, 21* (1993), 20–21.

Vygotsky, L.S. *Thought and Language*. Cambridge, Mass.: MIT Press, 1962.

Zucker, C. "Using Whole Language with Students Who Have Language and Learning Disabilities." *The Reading Teacher, 46* (May 1993): 660–669.

Part IV

Resources for Children's Literature

Chapter Eleven
A Reading and Resource Listing

Hannah Nuba
Siobhan O'Neil

Books for Children

The following is a selective and representative guide to over four hundred books chosen from the wealth of children's literature available today.

INFANTS AND TODDLERS

Ages 1 and Up

Baby Says. By John Steptoe. Illustrated by the author. New York: Lothrop, Lee & Shepard, 1988.

A perfect first book to share with a little one.

Fast Car. By Hannah Giffard. Illustrated by the author. New York: Tambourine, 1993.

Take a fast car or a slow tractor. Ride a noisy speed boat or a quiet canoe, and enjoy traveling across the pages.

Fiddle-I-Fee. A Farmyard Song for the Very Young. Adapted and illustrated by Melissa Sweet. Boston: Little, Brown, 1992.

A fresh and sparkling adaptation of a classic nursery rhyme.

Cindy Szekeres' Giggles. By Cyndy Szekeres. Illustrated by the author. New York: Golden Books, 1996.

Little ones will giggle their way through this happy book.

Hunky Dory Found It. By Katie Evans. Illustrated by Janet Morgan Stoeke. New York: Dutton, 1994.

Hunky Dory is a delightful little puppy who loves to find things even when they are not lost.

I Touch. By Rachel Isadora. Illustrated by the author. New York: Greenwillow, 1985.

Along with the companion books *I See* and *I Hear, I Touch* is perfect for babies.

James Balog's Animals A to Z. By James Balog. Photographs by the author. San Francisco: Chronicle, 1996.

Vivid, striking photographs make this a most appealing ABCs book.

Max's First Word. By Rosemary Wells. Illustrated by the author. New York: Dial, 1979.

In this humorous board book, Ruby is very patient with her little brother as she tries to teach him the correct words for a variety of things. Look for other Max books in the series.

One Little Kitten. By Tana Hoban. Photographs by the author. New York: Greenwillow, 1979.

A curious little kitten goes exploring—until it's time to get back to his mother and dinner! Lilting rhymes and great photographs.

1, 2, 3. By William Wegman. Photographs by the author. New York: Hyperion, 1995.

The author, a well-known photographer, has produced a wonderfully special counting book by having handsome weimaraners strike funny poses to delight the young reader.

Pat-a-Cake and Other Play Rhymes. Compiled by Joanna Cole and Stephanie Calmenson. Illustrated by Alan Tiegreen. New York: Morrow, 1992.

Lively collection of thirty favorite rhymes for baby and parent to enjoy.

Pat the Bunny. By Dorothy Kunhardt. Illustrated by the author. New York: Western, 1942.

In this beloved classic, Paul and Judy play peek-a-boo, smell flowers, look into the mirror, touch daddy's scratchy face, and, of course, pat the bunny. Two companion books, *Pat the Puppy* and *Pat the Cat,* are just as delightful.

Reindeer Baby. By Cynthia Alvarez. Illustrated by Julie Durrell. New York: Random House, 1995.

All about snow, holly leaves, and mistletoe, this book has many enjoyable tactile features, including the softest baby that little hands will want to touch. Part of the series More Fuzzy Chunky books, suiting a baby's need to touch and feel.

Richard Scarry's Best Word Book Ever. By Richard Scarry. Illustrated by the author. New York: Golden Press, 1963, revised edition 1980.

Detailed, appealing drawings fill the pages of this picture book, designed to encourage the child's language discovery.

Sesame Street Word Book. By Tom Leigh. Illustrated by the author. New York: Western, 1983.

Popular Sesame Street characters provide a familiar background for exploring the world of words.

Sleep Song. By Karen Ray. Illustrated by Rhonda Mitchell. New York: Orchard Books, 1995.

Baby uses playful delaying tactics to make "just-before-bed-time" last just a little longer.

Splish, Splash. By Lizi Boyd. Illustrated by the author. San Francisco: Chronicle, 1995.

Feel the rubber ducks, pat the soft towels, touch the cuddly pajamas. A perfect bath and bed story for the very young. *Fuzz and Fur* by the same author is an equally engaging book.

The Touch Me Book. By Pat and Eve Witte. Illustrated by Harlow Rockwell. New York: Golden Books, 1961.

A cheerful book that offers engaging tactile activities.

Where's Spot? By Eric Hill. Illustrated by the author. New York: Putnam, 1980.

What fun to join a mother dog in her search for her lost puppy! Children adore all books in the Spot series.

Wibbly Pig Makes Pictures. By Mick Inpen. Illustrated by the author. New York: Golden Books, 1995.

Little ones like seeing themselves in little Wibbly Pig's antics in this and all the enjoyable Wibbly Pig books.

Ages 2 and Up

Alfonse, Where Are You? By Linda Wikler. Illustrated by the author. New York: Crown, 1996.

Little Bird, a young duckling, and Alfonse, a gray goose, play hide-and-seek. But then Little Bird really disappears, and Alfonse can't find his friend. Children will love to help him, especially when Alfonse keeps missing Little Bird as the pages are turned.

Animals Should Definitely Not Wear Clothing. By Judi Barrett. Illustrated by Ron Barrett. New York: Atheneum, 1988.

A camel that wears hats? A walrus in a jacket? A giraffe with six neckties? Young children will giggle their way through the pages of this funny book. *Animals Should Definitely Not Act Like People* is an equally amusing companion volume.

Birthday Rhymes—Special Times. Selected by Bobbye S. Goldstein. Illustrated by Jose Aruego and Ariane Dewey. New York: Delacorte, 1993.

This appealing collection of verses from Dr. Seuss, Ogden Nash, and Karla Kuskin, among others, is sure to captivate the young birthday child and bring pleasure all year round.

Brown Cow, Green Grass, Yellow Mellow Sun. By Ellen B. Jackson. Illustrated by Victoria Raymond. New York: Hyperion, 1995.

Pleasing rhymes and illustrations modeled from clay make this a charming picture book.

Can't Sleep. By Chris Raschka. Illustrated by the author. New York: Orchard Books, 1965.

Little dog is snugly tucked in bed, and wide awake. But not for long! A soothing bedtime story for young children.

Close Your Eyes. By Jean Marzollo. Illustrated by Susan Jeffers. New York: Dial, 1978.

Bedtime with a gentle lullaby and beautiful illustrations.

Colors Everywhere. By Tana Hoban. Photographs by the author. New York: Greenwillow, 1994.

Clear photographs show children the riches of color in the world of nature. Look for other equally splendid books for young children by Tana Hoban.

Come Back, Puppies. By Jan Ormerod. Illustrated by the author. New York: Lothrop, Lee & Shepard, 1992.

A great way for little ones to play peekaboo and hide-and-seek.

Counting Cows. By Woody Jackson. Illustrated by the author. San Diego: Harcourt Brace Jovanovich, 1995.
> First there are ten cows and then there are none. A backward counting book with delightful illustrations.

Counting Our Way to Maine. By Maggie Smith. Illustrated by the author. New York: Orchard, 1995.
> This fun-filled count-along picture book captures all the pleasures and problems of a family on vacation.

Counting Wildflowers. By Bruce McMillan. Photographs by the author. New York: Lothrop, Lee & Shepard, 1986.
> A cheerful book that highlights American wildflowers in beautiful color photos.

Dancing Feet. By Charlotte Agell. Illustrated by the author. San Diego: Harcourt Brace Jovanovich, 1994.
> Busy little feet dance, skip, walk, and play around the world.

Edward Unready for School. By Rosemary Wells. Illustrated by the author. New York: Dial, 1995.
> The author of the engaging books about Max and Ruby, the adorable rabbit toddlers, here takes a sensitive look at a little bear who is just not ready to go into an unfamiliar situation. Cheerful illustrations enhance the text. Look for other Edward adventures in the series.

Freight Train. By Donald Crews. Illustrated by the author. New York: Greenwillow, 1978.
> All aboard! From city to country, day and night, a freight train speeds across the pages of this colorful book.

Frogs in Clogs. By Sheila White Samton. Illustrated by the author. New York: Crown, 1995.
> Green frogs wearing pink and orange clogs? Pink pigs eating purple figs and wearing brightly colored wigs? New surprises giggle after giggle.

Goodnight Moon. By Margaret Wise Brown. Illustrated by Clement Hurd. New York: Harper & Row, 1947.
> A little bunny helps the child gently float off to sleep in this delightful, all-time favorite bedtime classic.

"Hi, Pizza Man!" By Virginia Walter. Illustrated by Ponder Goembel. New York: Orchard Books, 1995.

> Vivian is starving, but where is that pizza man? Imaginative and funny.

Jump, Frog, Jump. By Robert Kalan. Illustrated by Byron Barton. New York: Greenwillow, 1981.

> Playful antics and cumulative rhymes to delight the young.

Kate Gleeson's Little Elephant Surprise. By Caroline Kenneth. Illustrated by Kate Gleeson. New York: Golden Books, 1996.

> Bubbly rhyming text follows little elephant on his special day right up to the surprise that awaits him.

Leonard. By Wolf Erlbruch. Illustrated by the author. New York: Orchard Books, 1995.

> Little Leonard loves dogs, but he is also a bit afraid of them. Then he has a special dream that makes all the difference.

Little Elephant. By Miela Ford. Photographs by Tana Hoban. New York: Greenwillow, 1994.

> A sweet story about a little elephant and his loving mother teamed with outstanding photographs.

Mary Had a Little Lamb. By Sarah Josepha Buell Hale. Illustrated by Salley Mavor. New York: Orchard Books, 1995.

> Since the poem was first published in 1830, children have continued to enjoy hearing about spunky Mary and her loyal but naughty little lamb.

One, Two, Three, Count with Me. By Catherine and Laurence Anholt. Illustrated by the authors. New York: Viking, 1993.

> Let's count everything we see from one little mouse to a million stars in the sky.

Pudmuddles. By Carol Beach York. Illustrated by Lisa Thiesing. New York: HarperCollins, 1993.

> What fun! Mrs. Pudmuddle likes to do everything backward, and children just love to follow her antics.

Quickly, Quigley. By Jeanne M. Gravois. Illustrated by Alison Hill. New York: Tambourine, 1993.

> Quigley is smaller and Quigley is slower than all the other pen-

guins at school, until that special day when Quigley outshines everyone!

Rhinos Who Surf. By Julie Mammano. Illustrated by the author. San Francisco: Chronicle, 1996.

A hilarious look at surfing rhinos.

The Snowy Day. By Ezra Jack Keats. Illustrated by the author. New York: Viking, 1962.

Little Peter stars in this absolutely perfect picture book that has remained as fresh and sparkling as when it was first published over thirty years ago. A must for every child's book shelf.

A Teeny Tiny Baby. By Amy Schwartz. Illustrated by the author. New York: Orchard Books, 1994.

A perfect introduction for an expectant sibling when a new baby joins the family. Lovely gouache paintings add to the enjoyment of this charming book.

Ten Little Rabbits. By Virginia Grossman. Illustrated by Sylvia Long. San Francisco: Chronicle, 1991.

Unique counting book that celebrates Native American culture.

Ten, Nine, Eight. By Molly Bang. Illustrated by the author. New York: Greenwillow, 1983.

In this special, warm picture book, a little boy and his loving father prepare for bedtime.

Ten Old Pails. By Nicholas Heller. Illustrated by Yossi Abolafia. New York: Greenwillow, 1994.

Who would want ten old pails? A creative and funny tale.

Twist with a Burger, Jitter with a Bug. By Linda Lowery. Illustrated by Pat Dypold. Boston: Houghton Mifflin, 1995.

Lively cut-paper collages go along with bubbly rhymes that will have little readers dancing.

The Very Hungry Caterpillar. By Eric Carle. Illustrated by the author. New York: Philomel, 1970.

A delicious picture book that follows a hungry caterpillar as he eats his way to becoming a beautiful butterfly

THE PRESCHOOL YEARS

Ages 3 and Up

Albert's Nap. By Michael Grejniec. Illustrated by the author. New York: North-South, 1995.

All Albert wants to do is take a little nap, but a pesky mosquito won't let him. A very funny story.

Alphabet City. By Stephen T. Johnson. Illustrated by the author. New York: Viking, 1995.

Look around you! There are alphabet letters everywhere in the city. Striking illustrations let this urban setting spring to life.

Anansi Goes Fishing. By Eric A. Kimmel. Illustrated by Janet Stevens. New York: Holiday, 1992.

In this amusing African folktale, a clever turtle outwits Anansi, the lovable but tricky spider whose schemes always have a way of catching up with him.

Anna's Special Present. By Yoriko Tsutsui. Illustrated by Akiko Hayashi. New York: Viking, 1983.

A companion book to *Anna's Secret Friend,* this is a realistic story about two young sisters and the special bond between them.

April Showers. By George Shannon. Illustrated by Jose Aruego and Ariane Dewey. New York: Greenwillow, 1995.

Young readers join gleeful frogs on a showery April day.

Astronauts Are Sleeping. By Natalie Standiford. Illustrated by Allen Garns. New York: Knopf, 1996.

What do astronauts dream about as they are spinning in outer space? An unusual bedtime story.

At the Zoo. By Douglas Florian. Illustrated by the author. New York: Greenwillow, 1992.

Lively pictures and lilting rhymes make this book like a great trip to the zoo

Away from Home. By Anita Lobel. Illustrated by the author. New York: Greenwillow, 1994.

A spectacular whirlwind tour that propels Adam and his friends through the alphabet from Amsterdam to Zaandam in alliterative fashion.

The Berenstain Bears and the Spooky Old Tree. By Stan and Janice Berenstain. Illustrated by the authors. New York: Beginner Books, 1978.

Inside and out, into, up, through, and around! Three delightful little bears explore an old tree and learn about spatial concepts. Children love to follow the adventures of the Berenstain Bears. Look for books for slightly older children by the same authors.

Blackboard Bear. By Martha G. Alexander. Illustrated by the author. New York: Dial, 1988.

A lonely little boy draws a picture of a bear on his chalkboard, and to his surprise the bear steps out to become his playmate. Look for other books in the series about a little boy and his imaginary friend.

Bread and Jam for Frances. By Russell Hoban. Illustrated by Lillian Hoban. New York: HarperCollins, 1964.

An irrepressible little badger wants to eat nothing else but bread and jam. There are other equally amusing books about Frances and her adventures.

Brown Bear, Brown Bear, What Do You See? By Bill Martin Jr. Illustrated by Eric Carle. New York: Henry Holt, 1967, 1992.

Beautiful twenty-fifth-anniversary edition of this well-loved classic.

Camel Caravan. By Bethany Roberts and Patricia Hubbell. Illustrated by Cheryl Munro Taylor. New York: Tambourine, 1996.

Five camels are tired of having to carry all those heavy packs across the desert and decide to do something about it in this adventurous story.

The Camel Who Took a Walk. By Jack Tworkov. Illustrated by Roger Duvoisin. New York: Dutton, 1951.

Going on a leisurely walk one morning, a stately camel is unaware that a crafty tiger is ready to pounce. Delightfully suspenseful!

Caps for Sale. By Esphyr Slobodkina. Illustrated by the author. New York: Harper & Row, 1947; New York: Scholastic, 1968.

A sleepy cap peddler is almost outsmarted by a playful group of little monkeys. A classic that has withstood the test of time.

Carnival. By M.C. Helldorfer. Illustrated by Dan Yaccarino. New York: Viking, 1996.

Filled with color and vitality, this picture book visits an old-fashioned carnival.

Chicken Soup with Rice: A Book of Months. By Maurice Sendak. Illustrated by the author. New York: Scholastic, 1962, 1991.

A sparkling story in rhyme about the perfect dish for each month in the year.

The Circus Baby. By Maud and Miska Petersham. Illustrated by the authors. New York: Macmillan, 1950.

Mother elephant decides that the time has come for baby elephant to learn good table manners. Of course the results are very funny, much to the pleasure of young readers.

Clifford, We Love You. By Norman Bridwell. Illustrated by the author. New York: Scholastic, 1994.

Clifford, a big shaggy dog, has entertained young children for over twenty-five years. Here, Clifford is sad and nothing will cheer him up until his owner, Aunt Elizabeth, writes him a happy song.

Cloudy with a Chance of Meatballs. Judi Barrett. Illustrated by Ron Barrett. Atheneum, 1978.

How wonderful! In the land of chew and swallow, all the food falls right from the skies.

Coconut Mon. By Linda Milstein. Illustrated by Cheryl Munro Taylor. New York: Tambourine, 1995.

A colorful book that dances with the lively rhythm of the Caribbean.

Corduroy. By Don Freeman. Illustrated by the author. New York: Viking, 1968.

An adorable little bear is discovered in a toy store by a loving little girl who finds a way to bring him home to be her very own.

The Cow Who Fell in the Canal. By Phyllis Krasilovsky. Illustrated by Peter Spier. Garden City, N.Y.: Doubleday, 1957/New York: Dell, 1993.

In this endearing classic, Hendrika, a very special cow, is tired of life in the country and longs to visit the city. After she falls into the canal her wish comes true.

Curious George. By H.A. Rey. Illustrated by the author. Boston: Houghton Mifflin, 1941.

> All about a little monkey who is sometimes just too curious for his own good. In this story, fortunately, the man in the yellow hat comes to the rescue. Generations of children have enjoyed this classic and many of the other stories about George.

Daddies: All About the Work They Do. By Janet Frank. Updated by Margo Lundell. Illustrated by Paul Meisel. New York: Golden Books, 1996.

> Just like mommies, daddies can have many different jobs, and children like learning about all the possibilities.

Daisy-Head Mayzie. By Dr. Seuss. Illustrated by the author. New York: Random House, 1994.

> Mayzie McGrew, this book's little heroine, suddenly sprouts a daisy right on top of her head, making her the center of much unwelcome attention. This story, based on a manuscript found among Dr. Seuss's papers, offers all the fun children have come to expect from his books.

The Day I Had to Play with My Sister. By Crosby Bonsall. Illustrated by the author. New York: Harper & Row, 1972.

> Little sister will not play by the rules, much to the chagrin of her older brother. Young readers will empathize and enjoy.

Diane Goode's Book of Silly Stories and Songs. By Diane Goode. Illustrated by the author. New York: Dutton, 1992.

> These silly, zany stories from all over the world make children giggle with glee.

Dinosaurs at the Supermarket. By Lindsay Camp. Illustrated by Clare Skilbeck. New York: Viking, 1993.

> While digging for buried treasure Laura and her imaginary crocodile friend discover a dinosaur bone. This winning tale takes the reader on a merry chase.

Discover the Seasons. By Diane Iverson. Illustrated by the author. Nevada City, Calif.: Dawn, 1996.

> The seasons are celebrated in this lovely, colorful book that fosters a love for nature in young children.

Don't Wake Up Mama! Another Five Little Monkeys Story. By Eileen Christelow. Illustrated by the author. New York: Clarion, 1992.

The five jolly characters are back with their antics in this cheerful story that sees them busily, but not very quietly, baking a birthday cake for their mother while she is asleep.

Ella's Trip to the Museum. By Elaine Clayton. Illustrated by the author. New York: Crown, 1996.

A hilarious class visit to the museum that the children will never forget.

Flying. By Donald Crews. Illustrated by the author. New York: Greenwillow, 1986.

Board the plane, tighten the seat belt, and take off! A lively mixture of text and pictures capture's the thrill of a first airplane flight.

Getting Used to Harry. By Cari Best. Illustrated by Diane Palmisciano. New York: Orchard, 1996.

A sparkling, wise, and very funny look at the changes, challenges, and pleasures of becoming a new family. Lively, humorous illustrations fully capture the charm and playfulness of this delightful story.

Going to the Zoo. By Tom Paxton. Illustrated by Karen Lee Smith. New York: Morrow 1996.

A classic song springs to life with playful rhymes and appealing illustrations.

Goldilocks and the Three Bears. Retold by Jonathan Langley. Illustrated by the author. New York: HarperCollins, 1993.

Charming, fresh retelling of a familiar fairy tale.

Goldilocks and the Three Bears. Retold by James Marshall. Illustrated by the author. New York: Dial, 1988.

The deliciously irreverent humor of the illustrations and the lighthearted text add a new sparkle to this familiar story.

Goody O' Grumpity. By Carol Ryrie Brink. Illustrated by Ashley Wolff. New York: North-South, 1994.

When Goody bakes a cake, everyone in the village comes for the wonderful smells, a lick, and a taste. Set in colonial times, this classic poem and authentic illustrations make for a delicious reading experience. A tempting recipe is included.

Grandfather's Journey. By Allen Say. Illustrated by the author. Boston: Houghton Mifflin, 1993.

Touching reminiscences that convey a family's love for their native country as well as their adopted one. Exquisite paintings enhance the poignant story.

The Grumpalump. By Sarah Hayes. Illustrated by Barbara Firth. New York: Clarion, 1990.

Page by page, children will try to guess just what a "Grumpalump" is.

Higgle Wiggle: Happy Rhymes. By Eve Merriam. Illustrated by Hans William. New York: Morrow, 1994.

Cheerful collection of hippity-hoppity verses.

I'll Be the Horse If You'll Play with Me. By Martha Alexander. Illustrated by the author. New York: Dial, 1975.

It's not always easy to be a middle child, and this charming book tells the story.

In the Back Seat. By Deborah Durland De Saix. Illustrated by the author. New York: Farrar, Straus & Giroux, 1993.

Jeffrey thinks car trips are boring, but his big sister knows how to change his mind. A whimsical and engaging adventure story.

In the Snow. By Huy Voun Lee. Illustrated by the author. New York: Henry Holt, 1995.

In sparkling, lyrical language and lively, cut-paper collage illustrations, this story tells of a warm mother–son relationship and the joys of passing on old and honored traditions.

Inch by Inch. By Leo Lionni. Illustrated by the author. New York: Astor-Honor, 1960.

A captive yet clever little worm manages his way to freedom, inch by inch. Imaginative text and glowing pictures.

Inside-Out Grandma: A Hanukkah Story. By Joan Rothenberg. Illustrated by the author. New York: Hyperion, 1995.

A warm family story all about Grandma's traditional potato pancakes (recipe included).

Jamaica's Find. By Juanita Havill. Illustrated by Anne Sibley O' Brien. Boston: Houghton Mifflin, 1986.

It was easy for Jamaica to bring to the lost and found a red cap she found in the park, but turning in a cuddly toy dog that was also lost was different. Wasn't it okay to keep him? An affectionate story with a very special ending.

Jump, Frog, Jump. By Robert Kalan. Illustrated by Byron Barton. New York: Greenwillow, 1981.

Cumulative, rhyming tale for the very young.

Just Look. By Tana Hoban. Photographs by the author. New York: Greenwillow, 1996.

Tana Hoban, the eminent photographer, transforms the unfamiliar into the familiar through die-cut pages that enchant and challenge as they conceal and reveal.

The Little Engine That Could. Retold by Watty Piper. Illustrated by George and Doris Hauman. New York: Platt and Munk, 1930, 1961.

All seems lost when the train that carries good things for children breaks down and is not able to go over the mountain. But, of course, Little Engine saves the day. A beloved classic.

Little Hobbin. By Theodor Storm. Illustrated by Lisbeth Zweger. Translated by Anthea Bell. New York: North-South, 1995.

Little Hobbin's big problem is not knowing when to stop and when enough is enough in this delightful cautionary tale.

The Little Red Hen. By Paul Galdone. Illustrated by the author. New York: Seabury Press, 1973.

Appealing classic about an industrious and wise little hen who finds the perfect way to teach her friends the value of sharing.

Madeline. By Ludwig Bemelmans. Illustrated by the author. New York: Simon & Schuster, 1939/New York: Viking, 1967.

Generations of children have loved Madeline, the irrepressible heroine of this wonderful classic. Look for other Madeline adventures.

Make Way for Ducklings. By Robert McCloskey. Illustrated by the author. New York: Viking, 1941, 1969.

Captivating classic about a delightful family of ducklings in search of new home.

Mama Coming and Going. By Judith Caseley. Illustrated by the author. New York: Greenwillow, 1994.

After Jenna's baby brother is born, Mama becomes very absent-minded. While she remembers to read Jenna a bedtime story, she forgets to defrost the chicken for dinner and other odd things. But where Jenna sees this as a chance to be the helpful big sister, Mama is fine again, "coming and going."

Mowing. By Jessie Haas. Illustrated by Jos. A. Smith. New York: Greenwillow, 1994.

Nora, a very special little girl, helps her grandfather mow the field, being very careful not to hurt the little animals that sometimes hide in the tall grass.

My Red Umbrella. By Robert Bright. Illustrated by the author. New York: Morrow, 1959.

It's raining! A sweet little girl's red umbrella keeps expanding so that everyone who needs shelter can get under it.

My Secret Place. By Erica Magnus. Illustrated by the author. New York: Lothrop, Lee & Shepard, 1994.

Lovely artwork enhances this gentle story about a child's first step to independence.

Ndito Runs. By Laurie Halse Anderson. Illustrated by Anita Van der Merwe. New York: Henry Holt, 1996.

In Kenya, school is miles away for many children. Ndito is one of them, as she runs past the thatch-covered homes in her village, down hills, through the grassland, past the water hole, and on to her beloved schoolhouse.

Neeny Coming, Neeny Going. By Karen English. Illustrated by Synthia Saint James. Mahwah, N.J.: BridgeWater Books, 1996.

Families change, but their closeness lasts forever. A sensitive story, set off the coast of South Carolina, that blends American and West African customs.

Pierre: A Cautionary Tale. By Maurice Sendak. Illustrated by the author. New York: Harper & Row, 1962, 1990.

Delightful rhymes and humorous illustrations about a willful little boy who learned to care. A classic loved by generations of young children.

A Pocket for Corduroy. By Don Freeman. Illustrated by the author. New York: Viking, 1978.

This follow-up to *Corduroy* brings along the same warmth and gentle humor that made this lovable bear so popular.

Red Light, Green Light. By Margaret Wise Brown. Illustrated by Leonard Weisgard. New York: Scholastic, 1992.

Still a favorite, this introduction to traffic lights was first published in 1944.

Red Light, Green Light, Mama and Me. By Cari Best. Illustrated by Niki Daly. New York: Orchard Books, 1995.

Going to the library is fun, but when your own mama is the children's librarian, well, what could be nicer? A charming story about a little girl's very special library day.

Sam and the Lucky Money. By Karen Chinn. Illustrated by Cornelius Van Wright and Ying-Hwa Hu. New York: Lee & Low, 1995.

Vivid watercolor paintings complete the charming picture that celebrates the sights and sounds of festive Chinatown and tells the story of a young boy at a Chinese New Year celebration.

A Song for Lena. By Hilary Horder Hippely. Illustrated by Leslie Baker. New York: Simon & Schuster, 1996.

A wonderful play of pretend between a loving mother and her little boy.

A Spark in the Dark. By Richard Tichnor and Jenny Smith. Illustrated by the authors. Nevada City, Calif.: Dawn, 1994.

Playful images tell the story "of a world that began with all little children as part of the plan. No matter the color, the shape big or small, the star loved them all."

Spider, Spider. By Kate Banks. Illustrated by George Hallensleben. New York: Farrar, Straus & Giroux, 1997.

It all started when Peter watched a spider crawl across the floor. A sweet story about the magic of make-believe.

The Tangerine Tree. By Regina Hanson. Illustrated by Harvey Stevenson. Saint Louis: Clarion, 1995.

Set in Jamaica, this is a warm family story filled with love and hope.

Taxi! Taxi! By Cari Best. Illustrated by Dale Gottlieb. Boston: Little, Brown, 1994.

Sundays belong to Tina and her Papi. That's the day he comes in his shining yellow taxi, and just the two of them spend the day together. A poignant story that radiates with tenderness and emotion. The delightful illustrations enrich the telling.

Tell Me a Story Mama. By Angela Johnson. Illustrated by David Soman. New York: Orchard Books, 1989.

A little girl loves to listen to stories, and no one tells them better than Mama. Complemented by detailed, charming illustrations, this story looks lovingly into the life of a warm and caring family.

This Is the Way We Eat Our Lunch: A Book about Children around the World. By Edith Baer. Illustrated by Steve Bjorkman. New York: Scholastic, 1995.

"Time for lunch! What will it be? Come along—let's taste and see!" A culinary journey in rhyme.

Waiting for Christmas. By Monica Greenfield. Illustrated by Jan Spivey Gilchrist. New York: Scholastic, 1996.

It's Christmastime—filled with snowflakes, sledding, presents, delicious food, good family, and lots of wonderful friends.

What's on the Menu? Food Poems. Selected by Bobbye S. Goldstein. Illustrated by Chris L. Demarest. New York: Viking, 1992.

Delicious collection of wonderful poems both children and adults enjoy!

When I'm Alone. By Carol Partridge Ochs. Illustrated by Vicki Jo Redenbaugh. Minneapolis: Carolrhoda, 1993.

Playful animal visitors and their little hostess create a bit of chaos in this counting book.

Ages 4 and Up

Alamo across Texas. By Jill Stover. Illustrated by the author. New York: Lothrop, Lee & Shepard, 1993.

Drought has come to the Lavaca River area, and Alamo, the alligator, has to move on. Bright pictures and happy rhymes follow Alamo in his search for a new home.

Amazing Grace. By Mary Hoffman. Illustrated by Caroline Binch. New York: Dial, 1991.

Grace loves to read stories and act them out. So, when her class plans to put on *Peter Pan,* Grace is sure she will get the leading role. Will she? A winsome story about a spirited, determined young girl.

Amos and Boris. By William Steig. Illustrated by the author. New York: Farrar, Straus & Giroux, 1971.

A touching, humorous story about the friendship between Amos, a seafaring mouse, and Boris, a whale.

Arthur Meets the President. By Marc Tolon Brown. Illustrated by the author. Boston: Little, Brown, 1991.

One of many titles in the popular Arthur series, lucky Arthur wins an essay contest, and along with all his classmates he is invited to the White House. A sparkling adventure with a happy ending.

Bad Day at Riverbend. By Chris Van Allsburg. Illustrated by the author. Boston: Houghton Mifflin, 1995.

What's going on in Riverbend? Lots of strange, mysterious things that need investigating have been happening in this small western town. The fun is in finding out!

Beach Feet. By Lynn Reiser. Illustrated by the author. New York: Greenwillow, 1996.

How many different kinds of feet can be found at the beach? A perfect combination of fact and fancy that invites many repeat readings.

A Bear for All Seasons. By Diane Marcial Fuchs. Illustrated by Kathryn Brown. New York: Henry Holt, 1995.

It's wintertime and bear is just about ready to drift into a long nap, when his friend Fox stops by for a visit. They talk about the wonders of the seasons and what they like best about each.

In the end they agree that having a good friend is best of all.

Big Brave Brother Ben. By Kara May. Illustrated by Gus Clarke. New York: Lothrop, Lee & Shepard, 1991.

Ben isn't afraid of spiders, snakes, or even tigers. But there is something that does scare Ben, and only his little sister knows his secret. A warm and sensitive story.

Big Meeting. By Dee Parmer Woodtor. Illustrated by Dolores Johnson. New York: Atheneum, 1996.

This joyous book conveys a powerful sense of home and family.

The Biggest Bear. By Lynd Ward. Illustrated by the author. Boston: Houghton Mifflin, 1952, 1980.

Johnny wanted a bearskin for his barn and set out to find himself a really big bear in this timeless classic.

The Butterfly Seeds. By Mary Watson. Illustrated by the author. New York: Tambourine, 1995.

A parting gift of magical seeds makes moving to a new country and leaving his grandfather behind a less painful experience for Jake.

Calling the Doves. By Juan Felipe Herrera. Illustrated by Elly Simmons. San Francisco: Children's Book Press, 1995.

Touchingly told by the author, one of Mexico's most prominent poets, this glowing story recalls a childhood filled with family, warmth, song, and celebration.

The Case of the Cat's Meow. By Crosby Bonsall. Illustrated by the author. New York: Harper & Row, 1965.

An irresistible "I Can Read Mystery," filled with humor and real suspense.

The Cat in the Hat. By Dr. Seuss. Illustrated by the author. New York: Random House, 1957.

Children continue to delight in the absurdities spun in the story rhymes by Dr. Seuss.

Cinderella. Retold by Barbara Karlin. Illustrated by James Marshall. Boston: Little, Brown, 1989.

In this new version of the classic fairy tale, a delightful difference awaits the young reader.

George and Martha. By James Marshall. Illustrated by the author. Boston: Houghton Mifflin, 1972.

Five sweet stories about two kind-hearted hippos who know what friendship is all about.

Geraldine First. By Holly Keller. Illustrated by the author. New York: Greenwillow, 1996.

Another adventure about Geraldine, a charming little pig. In this story, her little brother keeps following her everywhere, making it a problem waiting to be resolved. Gentle story and sweet illustrations.

Go Away, Big Green Monster! By Ed Emberley. Illustrated by the author. Boston: Little, Brown, 1992.

Make the monster disappear by simply turning the page. A delightfully innovative book that lets the young reader be in control of the bad guys.

Going Back Home: An Artist Returns to the South. By Toyomi Igus. Illustrated by Michelle Wood. San Francisco: Children's Book Press, 1996.

Lovely story that touchingly depicts the experiences of a turn-of-the-century sharecropping family.

Good-bye House. By Robin Ballard. Illustrated by the author. New York: Greenwillow, 1994.

It's moving day and time to say good-bye to the old house. A reassuring story for young readers.

Grandpa's Hotel. By Riki Levinson. Illustrated by David Soman. New York: Orchard Books, 1995.

Sixteen cousins—all spending the summer at Grandpa's Hotel in the mountains! A story filled with family, fun, and love.

The Great Turtle Drive. By Steve Sanfield. Illustrated by Dirk Zimmer. New York: Knopf, 1996.

Humorous tall tale about an enterprising cowboy.

Happy Adoption Day! Lyrics by John McCutcheon. Illustrated by Julie Paschkis. Boston: Little, Brown, 1996.

A bright and cheerful story about a very special birthday!

Hector's New Sneakers. By Amanda Vesey. Illustrated by the author. New York: Viking, 1993.

Hector, a young crocodile, is not very happy with his new sneakers until some bad boys try to take them away from him. A warm story about being different.

How to Make an Apple Pie and See the World. By Marjorie Priceman. Illustrated by the author. New York: Knopf, 1994.

Tasty tale about a determined little baker.

I Don't Want to Go to Camp. By Eve Bunting. Illustrated by Maryann Cocca-Leffler. Honesdale, Pa.: Boyds Mills, 1996.

Reassuring picture book for little would-be campers.

I Spy School Days: A Book of Picture Riddles. Riddles by Jean Marzollo. Photographs by Walter Wick. New York: Scholastic, 1995.

This dazzling picture book is the sixth in an outstanding series.

I Will Go with My Family to Grandma's. By Riki Levinson. Illustrated by the author. New York: Dutton, 1986.

In this engaging, innovative, turn-of-the-century story, five young cousins go to visit grandma's house.

I'll Catch the Moon. By Nina Crews. Photographs by the author. New York: Greenwillow, 1996.

Serene photo-collage images lead into a dreamlike journey of discovery.

In a Circle Long Ago: A Treasury of Native Lore from North America. Retold by Nancy Van Laan. Illustrated by Lisa Desimini. New York: Apple Soup Books, 1995.

Selected and retold especially for young children, this rich anthology celebrates the earth's bounty and the value of all living things.

In Rosa's Mexico. By Campbell Geeslin. Illustrated by Andrea Arroyo. New York: Knopf, 1996.

Little Rosa takes the young reader to Mexico, her beautiful homeland.

In the Snow: Who's Been Here? By Lindsay B. George. Illustrated by the author. New York: Greenwillow, 1995.

Follow the animal's tracks in the snow and discover the clues that reveal its identity. A unique book that's informative and enjoyable.

Inner Chimes: Poems on Poetry. Selected by Bobbye Goldstein. Illustrated by Jane Breskin Zalben. Honesdale, Pa: Wordsong, Boyds Mills, 1992.

Featuring such renowned children's writers as Lee Bennett Hopkins, Eleanor Farjeon, Eve Merriam, Lillian Moore, and others, this delightful book is a celebration of the magic of poetry.

Ira Says Good-by. By Bernard Waber. Illustrated by the author. Boston: Houghton Mifflin, 1988.

Ira is sad because his best friend is moving away in this comforting story about separation and friendship.

Jennifer's Room. By Peter Utton. Illustrated by the author. New York: Orchard Books, 1995.

While waiting for her mother to call her for dinner, Jennifer reads a story in her room. But then, all sorts of mysterious things begin to happen. Playful text and whimsical illustrations.

Jigsaw Jackson. By David F. Birchman. Illustrated by Daniel San Souci. New York: Lothrop, Lee & Shepard, 1996.

Meet J.J. Jackson, a jigsaw champion like no other. Even the president invites him to come to Washington to display his talents.

A Kiss for Little Bear. By Else Holmelund Minarik. Illustrated by Maurice Sendak. New York: Harper & Row, 1968.

In this tender story a kiss is passed to grandmother, to hen, to cat, to skunk, and eventually back to little bear. There are many other Little Bear stories to delight young readers.

Last Dragon. By Susan Miho Nunes. Illustrated Chris K. Skoentpiet. New York: Clarion Books, 1995.

Peter Chang is not very happy when he has to spend the summer with his great-aunt, who lives in Chinatown. But after he meets a sad and lonely dragon, his summer becomes an amazing adventure.

Lilly's Purple Plastic Purse. By Kevin Henkes. Illustrated by the author. New York: Greenwillow, 1996.

> Lilly the little mouse is back, to the delight of her young fans. In this story, Lilly loves school and everything about it, except when she has to wait her turn at sharing time!

The Little Ballerina. By Katherine Ross. Illustrated by Heidi Petach. New York: Random House, 1996.

> Little girls and boys who dream about becoming ballet dancers will be inspired by this story's little ballerina's determination to do well in the upcoming dance recital. Includes ballet terms, a pronunciation guide, and clear illustrations of ballet steps.

Little Sister and the Month Brothers. Retold by Beatrice Schenk De Regniers. Illustrated by Margot Tomes. New York: Seabury Press, 1976.

> A Slavic story retold with humor and style.

The Magic Fan. By Keith Baker. Illustrated by the author. San Diego: Harcourt Brace Jovanovich, 1989.

> None of the people who live in Yoshi's village like his magic bridge until it saves them from a terrible tidal wave. Beautiful illustrations go with this gentle story.

Mouse TV. By Matt Novak. Illustrated by the author. New York: Orchard Books, 1994.

> One day the television breaks down, upsetting the whole mouse family. What to do? Children will happily respond to the story's humor and lively cartoons.

Moving Day. By Robert Kalan. Illustrated by Yossi Abolafia. New York: Greenwillow, 1996.

> A gentle story about a little hermit crab anxious to find a new home.

Officer Buckle and Gloria. By Peggy Rathmann. Illustrated by the author. New York: Putnam, 1995.

> This delightful 1995 Caldecott Medal winner tells about Officer Buckle and his very wise dog, Gloria, who knows how to inspire children.

One Up, One Down. By Carol Snyder. Illustrated by Maxie Chambliss. New York: Atheneum, 1995.

> Being a big sister to twin brothers is not always easy. But Kathie likes to help. A humorous story with a gentle lesson.

The Patchwork Quilt. By Valerie Flournoy. Illustrated by Jerry Pinkney. New York: Dial, 1985.

> Captured in this touching story is the love and understanding between little Tanya and her treasured grandmother, as both work together on the quilt of family memories. Beautiful illustrations complete the warm portrait.

Quail Song: A Pueblo Indian Tale. Adapted by Valerie Scho Carey. Illustrated by Ivan Barnett. New York: Putnam, 1990.

> A Pueblo Indian story about a gentle quail and an arrogant coyote.

Red Riding Hood. Retold by James Marshall. Illustrated by the author. New York: Dial, 1987.

> A fresh interpretation of an old classic, complete with wonderfully wacky illustrations.

Reuben and the Fire. By Merle Good. Illustrated by P. Buckley Moss. Intercourse, Pa.: Good Books, 1993.

> Stunning illustrations and a lively text introduce young children to the world of the Amish.

Riddle-icious. By J. Patrick Lewis. Illustrated by Debbie Tilley. New York: Knopf, 1996.

> Real treat for kids who love riddles and puzzles.

Slumber Party. By Judith Caseley. Illustrated by the author. New York: Greenwillow, 1996.

> It's Zoe's birthday, and all her friends are invited to a slumber party. But at bedtime some strange things begin to happen. Sweet and funny.

Ten Flashing Fireflies. By Philemon Sturges. Illustrated by Anna Vojtech. New York: North-South, 1995.

> Ten fireflies illuminate the summer night, but when they are captured by two admiring children, their lights go out. A lovely story that shows that only free fireflies can shine.

Timothy Too! By Charlotte Zolotow. Illustrated by Ruth Robbins. Boston: Houghton Mifflin, 1986.

Being excluded from an older brother's play is troubling, but in this story, the problem is sensitively and gently resolved.

Titch and Daisy. By Pat Hutchins. Illustrated by the author. New York: Greenwillow, 1996.

Children know Titch from other stories and will be glad to welcome him back. In this story Titch is an unhappy party guest because his best friend, Daisy, is nowhere to be found. Of course in the end, the friends are reunited, just in time to join the fun.

Tomorrow's Alphabet. By George Shannon. Illustrated by Donald Crews. New York: Greenwillow, 1995.

Twenty-six surprises await the young reader in this alphabet book with a twist.

Tonio's Cat. By Mary Calhoun. Illustrated by Edward Martinez. New York: Morrow, 1996.

More than anything, Tonio misses Cazador, the dog he had to leave in Mexico when his family moved to California. And being new at school, without friends, doesn't make things any easier. But then one day, a sadly neglected, hungry stray cat jumps out of a garbage can and into his life. Glowing illustrations and sensitive text, interwoven with bilingual conversations, make this a heartwarming book.

White Socks Only. By Evelyn Coleman. Illustrated by Tyrone Geter. Morton Grove, Ill.: Whitman, 1996.

A deeply stirring story about a brave, intelligent girl during the time when bigots still ruled Mississippi.

Ages 5 and Up

The Ballad of the Pirate Queens. By Jane Yolen. Illustrated by David Shannon. San Diego: Harcourt Brace Jovanovich, 1995.

Dramatic illustrations accompany this action-packed poem about Anne Bonney and Mary Reade, who were real seafaring pirates in the 1700s.

The Ballot Box Battle. By Emily Arnold McCully. Illustrated by the author. New York: Knopf, 1996.

Realistic, appealing depiction of Elizabeth Cady Stanton's struggle in 1880 to win women's right to vote, and a little girl who bravely joins her.

Boundless Grace. By Mary Hoffman. Illustrated by Caroline Binch. New York: Dial, 1995.

Warm emotions glow in this delightful sequel to *Amazing Grace.* In this story, Grace visits her father in Africa and learns all about the value of strong family relationships.

Cat and Rat: The Legend of the Chinese Zodiac. By Ed Young. Illustrated by the author. New York: Henry Holt, 1995.

How were the twelve animals of the Chinese calendar chosen? An interesting story enriched by outstanding illustrations and a detailed chart of the Chinese zodiac.

The Dream Jar. By Bonnie Pryor. Illustrated by Mark Graham. New York: Morrow, 1996.

A story about Valentine, a caring little girl who helps make her Russian immigrant family's American dream come true. Graceful narrative interwoven with beautifully constructed illustrations.

Follow the Dream. By Peter Sis. Illustrated by the author. New York: Knopf, 1991.

Fact and legend combine to tell the story of Christopher Columbus. Lavish illustrations of maps and ship cross-sections and a travel log bring added energy to the text.

The Girl Who Loved Coyotes: Stories of the Southwest. By Nancy Wood. Illustrated by Diana Bryer. New York: Morrow, 1995.

The American Southwest is the linking land of Native American Spanish and Anglo Cultures. Here are twelve lively stories that capture the timeless spirit.

The Golden Goose. By the Brothers Grimm. Retold by Uri Shulevitz. Illustrated by the author. New York: Farrar, Straus & Giroux, 1995.

Fresh version of this traditional tale about a simple boy and the goose that brings him luck and fortune.

Haystack. By Bonnie Geisert and Arthur Geisert. Illustrated by the authors. Boston: Houghton Mifflin, 1995.

Absorbing account of the role of a prairie haystack in the life of a farm. Illustrations are clear and illuminating.

I Meant to Tell You. By James Stevenson. Illustrated by the author. New York: Greenwillow, 1996.

A warm and touching autobiographical look back to yesteryear.

I Spy a Freight Train: Transportation in Art. Devised and selected by Lucy Micklethwait. New York: Greenwillow, 1996.

See the stunning paintings found on each page of this extraordinary picture book and "spy" a car, a ship, an airplane, a horse, a rowboat, a sleigh, a wagon, a camel, a bicycle, a freight train, a hot-air balloon, a baby carriage, and even an elephant!

The Inside-Outside Book of Libraries. By Julie Cummins. Illustrated by Roxi Munro. New York: Dutton Books, 1996.

From a simple bookshelf in a child's home to the splendor of the Library of Congress in Washington, D.C., this fascinating, informative book takes the reader—young or old—"inside-outside" the world of books and libraries. The sparkling illustrations greatly enhance the enjoyment of this outstanding book.

Jim and the Beanstalk. By Raymond Briggs. Illustrated by the author. New York: Putnam, 1970.

This truly hilarious version of an old favorite is designed to have readers giggle with pleasure. Briggs's illustrations brim with humor and provide the perfect backdrop for this jolly retelling with a zany twist.

The Legend of the Bluebonnet: An Old Tale of Texas. By Tomie de Paola. Illustrated by the author. New York: Putnam, 1983.

Based on Comanche Indian lore, this touching story tells about a little girl named She-Who-Is-Alone and how her brave actions saved her people.

Market! By Ted Lewin. Illustrated by the author. New York: Lothrop, Lee & Shepard, 1996.

People from all over the world come to market to sell what they grow, catch, or make or to buy what other people have to offer. A palette of vivid colors makes the story spring to life.

A Million Fish . . . More or Less. By Patricia C. McKissack. Illustrated by Dena Schutzer. New York: Knopf, 1992.

An amusing tall tale about "one that got away."

The Mud Pony: A Traditional Skidi Pawnee Tale. By Caron L. Cohen. Illustrated by Shonto Begay. New York: Scholastic, 1988.

Touching story about a boy too poor to ever hope to have a pony of his own but who grows up to become chief to his people.

Mufaro's Beautiful Daughters: An African Tale. By John Steptoe. Illustrated by the author. New York: Lothrop, Lee & Shepard, 1987.

A memorable modern fable, enhanced by stunning illustrations.

My First Muppet Dictionary. Edited by Louise Gikow, Justine Korman, and Rita Rosenkranz. Designed by Tom Cooke. New York: Western, 1992.

Buoyant dictionary featuring the popular muppet characters, designed to motivate young children to take an interactive interest in the spoken and printed word.

Night Visitors. By Ed Young. Illustrated by the author. New York: Philomel, 1995.

Ho Kuam dreams of spending time in the busy world of ants so he can learn how they really live. When his wish comes true, he is able to save these tiny, industrious creatures from an evil enemy.

Not Now, Sara! By Hannelore Voight. Translated by J. Alison James. Illustrated by Oliver Corthey and Nicolas Fossati. New York: North-South, 1995.

Sara's painting was voted best in her class. Naturally she can hardly wait to take it home and show it to her family. But mother is busy with baby, father is still at work, and even her best friend is not around. A sensitive story which illustrates that patience will bring rewards.

Onions and Garlic: An Old Tale. By Eric A. Kimmel. Illustrated by Katya Arnold. New York: Holiday House, 1996.

Everyone thought of poor Getzel as the fool of the family until the day he went off to trade onions and garlic and came back with diamonds. A sparkling folktale that reminds children not to prejudge unkindly.

Puzzles. By Dava Walker. Illustrated by Cornelius Van Wright and Ying-Hwa Hu. Durham, N.C.: Lollipop Power, 1996.

Touching story about a brave young girl who learns to face the reality of sickle-cell disease with the help of a loving, supportive family.

Radio Boy. By Sharon Phillips Denslow. Illustrated by Alec Gillman. New York: Simon & Schuster, 1995.

Captivating and entertaining story about the boyhood of Nathan B. Stubblefield, the inventor of the wireless telephone, which eventually became known as the radio.

The Raggly, Scraggly, No-Soap, No-Scrub Girl. By David F. Birchman. Illustrated by Guy Porfirio. New York: Lothrop, Lee & Shepard, 1995.

All about a little girl who comes to visit a family she has never met and instantly creates all sorts of problems. She has no manners, and although covered with dust and dirt, she clearly shuns soap and water. A most appealing folktale.

Roger Tory Peterson's ABC of Birds: A Book for Little Birdwatchers. Illustrations and photographs by Roger Tory Peterson. New York: Universe, 1995.

A fascinating first introduction to birds and bird-watching.

Room of Mirrors. By Nomi Joval. Illustrated by Luszio Kubiny. Fort Lee, N.J.: Wonder Well, 1991.

An engaging blend of friendship, cooperation and the pleasure of curiosity.

Roses Are Pink, Your Feet Really Stink. By Diane De Groat. Illustrated by the author. New York: Morrow, 1996.

When Gilbert sends two, less-than-nice valentines to his classmates, his prank brings about the expected uproar. Will everyone in his class stay angry at him? A warm and funny book about forgiveness and friendship. The illustrations extend the humor of the story.

Running the Road to ABC. By Denize Lauture. Illustrated by Reynold Ruffins. New York: Simon & Schuster, 1996.

In this beautifully told tale, based on the author's own childhood in Haiti, nothing will keep the children from going to school, even if it means having to get up before dawn and dashing off into the darkness. Reynold Ruffins's stunning illustrations bring extraordinary splendor to this poetic story.

Tar Beach. By Faith Ringgold. Illustrated by the author. New York: Crown, 1991.

Originally written by the author for her story quilt, this gentle weave of fiction, autobiography, and African history results in pure magic.

Yard Sale. By James Stevenson. Illustrated by the author. New York: Greenwillow, 1996.

What a shopping event! The strange items on sale include a toothless comb, a clock without hands, a broken accordion, and a really ugly footstool. But treasures all! A page-turner that will have children agreeing that this is a yard sale like no other.

THE PRIMARY YEARS

Ages 6 and Up

Bedtime for Frances. By Russell Hoban. Illustrated by Garth Williams. New York: Harper & Row, 1960.

It's bedtime, and Frances, the irrepressible little badger, thinks up all sorts of delaying tactics. *Bread and Jam for Frances* and *A Bargain for Frances* are equally enjoyable books in the series.

Clean House. By Jessie Haas. Illustrated by Yossi Abolafia. New York: Greenwillow, 1996.

Company is coming, and Tess can hardly wait until Aunt Alice and cousin Kate arrive. Of course mother wants the house to be just perfect, so everyone helps in the cleaning—even the pets. A lighthearted, very amusing look at a familiar situation.

Cupid and Psyche. By M. Charlotte Craft. Illustrated by K.Y. Craft. New York: Morrow, 1996.

Based on the beautiful Greek myth, the story is told with stunning illustrations and clear, distinctive text.

Day at Damp Camp. By George Ella Lyon. Illustrated by Peter Catalanotto. New York: Orchard Books, 1996.

> Rich, lush illustrations and playful rhymes combine to tell of the many delights of summer at camp.

Dragon's Fat Cat. By Dav Pilkey. Illustrated by the author. New York: Orchard Books, 1992.

> Rib-tickling tale about a dragon who learns what is involved in cat care.

Emeka's Gift: An African Counting Story. By Ifeoma Onyefulu. Illustrated by the author. New York: Cobblehill, 1995.

> Superb photographs depict Nigerian customs and culture as seen through the eyes of Emeka, a young Nigerian, as he travels to his grandmother's house.

The Fiddle Ribbon. By Margo Lemieux. Illustrated by Francis Livingston. Parsippany, N.J.: Silver Burdett, 1996.

> Jenny and Jimmy are not enthusiastic about having to spend the whole summer helping Grandma and Grandpa work their farm. And at first things are as bad as they feared—until Grandpa brings out the fiddle that Grandma had brought long ago from far away. Gentle illustrations highlight this tender story.

Good Driving, Amelia Bedelia. By Herman Parish. Illustrated by Lynn Sweat. New York: Greenwillow, 1995.

> Much to the delight of her young fans, America's favorite housekeeper is back with all her flair for misinterpretations and mix-ups.

A Helpful Alphabet of Friendly Objects. By John Updike. Photographs by David Updike. New York: Knopf, 1995.

> The well-known author takes young readers on a witty, inventive trip through the alphabet. Photographs enhance this entertaining book.

Henry and Mudge and the Bedtime Thumps: The Ninth Book of Their Adventures. By Cynthia Rylant. Illustrated by Sucie Stevenson. New York: Bradbury Press, 1991.

> Children love to read about Henry and his very large dog Mudge and follow all the adventures in the series. In this story Henry is

worried that when Grandma comes to visit, she won't like Mudge.

I Is for India. By Prodeepta Das. Photographs by the author. Parsippany, N.J.: Silver Burdett, 1996.

Alphabetical introduction to India showing the country in all its dazzling diversity, from rice fields to snow-clad mountains, from sleepy villages to vibrant urban centers.

Juma and the Honey Guide: An African Tale. By Robin Bernard. Illustrated by Nneka Bennett. Parsippany, N.J.: Silver Burdett, 1996.

Interwoven with a sprinkling of Swahili words and vivid illustrations, this fact-based story makes fascinating reading.

The Little House. By Virginia L. Burton. Illustrated by the author. Boston: Houghton Mifflin, 1942.

A splendid classic story about a little house in the country that over the years is witness to the many changes that surround it.

The Magic School Bus Lost in the Solar System. By Joanna Cole. Illustrated by Bruce Degen. New York: Scholastic, 1990.

Again, Ms. Frizzle, the most exuberant teacher ever, is off on another adventure with the children in her class. This time they visit the planets. As with the other titles in the series, basic scientific facts join a fun-filled fantasy.

Moon Song. By Byrd Baylor. Illustrated by Ronald Himler. New York: Scribner, 1982.

Touching Pima Indian legend that explains why coyote children gather in the night and sing to the moon.

A Mouse in the House. By Gerda Wagener. Illustrated by Uli Waas. New York: North-South, 1995.

Socks the cat is so proud to have been able to catch a mouse that he brings his trophy right into the house for all the family to admire—with very funny results!

Old Salt, Young Salt. By Jonathan London. Illustrated by Todd L.W. Doney. New York: Lothrop, Lee & Shepard, 1996.

An exciting adventure story filled with warmth and humor that tells of the special bond between a boy and his father.

Pamela's First Musical. By Wendy Wasserstein. Illustrated by Andrew Jackson. New York: Hyperion, 1996.

It's Pamela's ninth birthday, and her elegant, glamorous Aunt Louise takes her to see her first musical. A sparkling story about a very special day.

Patrick Doyle Is Full of Blarney. By Jennifer Armstrong. Illustrated by Krista Brauckmann-Towns. New York: Random House, 1996.

The year is 1915 and Europe is at war, but in the United States the big story is baseball. A lively book about a feisty ten-year-old, baseball, and bullies. Much Irish flavor and charm, as well as interesting historical details about the era.

Schnorky the Wave Puncher. By Jeff Raglus. Illustrated by the author. New York: Crown, 1996.

Funky illustrations and funny text say, convincingly, that it's fine to be a nonconformist.

Spring: A Haiku Story. Selected by George Shannon. Illustrated by Malcah Zeldis. New York: Greenwillow, 1996.

Graceful introduction to haiku, as two children take a walk across a rural setting in early spring. Exquisite illustrations add to the enjoyment of the poetry.

Ages 7 and Up

Amber Brown Goes Fourth. By Paula Danziger. Illustrated by Tony Ross. New York: Putnam, 1995.

Fans of plucky Amber Brown have enjoyed her spirited exploits in her third-grade class, and will be equally delighted with her latest adventure in the series.

Andrew Wants a Dog. By Steven Kroll. Illustrated by Molly Delaney. New York: Hyperion, 1992.

More than anything in the world, Andrew wants a dog, but unhappily his father says "no." A charming story about a resourceful little boy who finds a most creative way to change his father's mind.

The Banshee Train. By Odds Bodkin. Illustrated by Ted Rose. New York: Clarion, 1995.

Steeped in rich Irish folk tradition, this captivating story tells about Irish immigrants who help build America's railways. Powerful illustrations and superb text make this a fascinating historical tale.

Beware the Mare. By Jessie Haas. Illustrated by Martha Haas. New York: Greenwillow, 1993.

Lilly loves her beautiful new bay mare—a present from Grandpa. She learns how to take good care of the horse, who in turn learns to trust Lilly. Still, Gramp is uneasy. And why would a mare this perfect be called "Beware"? This is a gripping tale for young readers.

Cars and How They Go. By Joanna Cole. Illustrated by Gail Gibbons. New York: Crowell, 1983.

A fascinating and authentic book for curious future young drivers that invites looking under the hood of a car to see what really makes the wheels go 'round.

Earth, Fire, Water, Air. By Mary Hoffman. Illustrated by Jane Ray. New York: Dutton, 1995.

Mesmerizing myths, legends, and stories from around the world to hold young readers spellbound.

Emily and Alice Again. By Joyce Champion. Illustrated by Sucie Stevenson. San Diego: Gulliver Books, 1995.

Three charming short stories about the joys and challenges of being best friends.

A Fly in the Sky. By Kristin Joy Pratt. Illustrated by the author. Nevada City, Calif.: Dawn, 1996.

An engaging, joyful exploration into the lives of birds, insects, and other flying creatures.

For Laughing Out Loud: Poems to Tickle Your Funnybone. Selected by Jack Prelutsky. Illustrated by Marjorie Priceman. New York: Knopf, 1991.

Just as the title promises, this collection of poems invites giggles and merriment.

George Washington's Mother. By Jean Fritz. Illustrated by DyAnne DiSalvo-Ryan. New York: Grosset & Dunlap, 1992.

A warm and unusual story about Mary Ball Washington, her family, her famous son, and the interesting times during which they lived.

Harry's Helicopter. By Joan Anderson. Illustrated by George Ancona. New York: Morrow, 1990.
Harry goes way up in the sky with a big, beautiful imaginary helicopter.

Homeless. By Bernard Wolf. Photographs by the author. New York: Orchard Books, 1995.
Poignant, heartbreaking, yet inspiring and optimistic story about eight-year-old Mikey and his family as they leave their bleak emergency shelter and move on to the caring environment of an urban family center. Although life is hard, Mikey is determined to grow up and "be somebody." The author has created a strong and realistic portrait of urban homelessness.

Martin Luther King. By Rosemary L. Bray. Illustrated by Malcah Zeldis. New York: Greenwillow, 1995.
Color-drenched folk art paintings enhance this fascinating biography of the revered African-American civil rights leader.

Marvelous Marvin and the Pioneer Ghost. By Bonnie Pryor. Illustrated by Melissa Sweet. New York: Morrow, 1995.
Marvin Freemont and his friends spin an exciting, suspenseful yarn about what happened on a spring vacation.

Muggie Maggie. By Beverly Cleary. Illustrated by Kay Life. New York: Morrow, 1990.
Young readers always welcome books by Beverly Cleary. In this amusing and realistic story, Maggie Schultz, a third-grader, decides that learning cursive writing is not necessary for a girl who knows how to use a computer.

Night of the Full Moon. By Gloria Whelan. Illustrated by Leslie Bowman. New York: Knopf, 1993.
On a still, moonlit night, Libby visits her friend Fawn, a Potawatomi Native American. But this friendly visit soon turns into a nightmare when cruel soldiers kidnap the girls. A riveting page-turner.

The Ocean of Story: Fairy Tales from India. Selection and notes by
Neil Philip. Retold by Caroline Ness. Illustrated by Jacqueline Mair.
New York: Lothrop, Lee & Shepard, 1995.

> A twelfth-century story in Sanskrit is just one of the many un-
> usual tales in this collection filled with magic and splendor.

A School for Pompey Walker. By Michael Rosen. Illustrated by Aminah
Brenda Lynn Robinson. San Diego: Harcourt Brace Jovanovich,
1995.

> Based on a true event, this story is about a courageous slave
> whose passion for education leads to his freedom and to the
> establishment of a school for young, disadvantaged children.
> Taut and well-crafted.

School's Out. By Johanna Hurwitz. Illustrated by Sheila Hamanaka.
New York: Morrow, 1991.

> Lucas Cott is not happy when he finds out that his mother has
> hired a babysitter over the summer to take care of him and his
> two-year-old twin brothers. An amusing and insightful story.

Taking Care of the Earth: Kids in Action. By Laurence Pringle. Illustrated by Bobbie Moore. Honesdale, Pa.: Boyds Mills, 1996.

> This excellent book highlights the work accomplished by chil-
> dren all over the world as they strive to take care of our planet.
> Perfect reading for young environmentalists.

Tanya's Reunion. By Valerie Flournoy. Illustrated by Jerry Pinkney.
New York: Dial, 1995.

> Fine pencil and watercolor illustrations combine to bring a warm
> picture of Tanya, a young girl and a family reunion that does
> not turn out as expected. A touching sequel to the award-win-
> ning *The Patchwork Quilt.*

The Token Gift. By Hugh William McKibbon. Illustrated by Scott
Cameron. Toronto: Annick/Firefly Books, 1996.

> Based on a Persian legend, this is the story of Mohan, who,
> inspired by his grandfather's many old army stories, creates a
> board game that is enjoyed even by the king of the land. An
> unusual book that will have young readers fully fascinated as
> the mathematical puzzle of the story unfolds.

Why Did the Chicken Cross the Road? And Other Riddles, Old and New. By Joanna Cole and Stephanie Calmenson. Illustrated by Alan Tiegreen. New York: Morrow, 1994.

> Assortment of over two hundred riddles to amuse and delight riddle fans.

Wilma Unlimited: How Wilma Rudolf Became the World's Fastest Woman. By Kathleen Krull. Illustrated by David Diaz. San Diego: Harcourt Brace Jovanovich, 1996.

> Interesting and inspiring story of Wilma Rudolf, an American runner who won three gold medals at the Olympic Games.

Ages 8 and Up

The Accidental Witch. By Anne Mazer. Illustrated by the author. New York: Hyperion, 1995.

> From the time she was four years old, Phoebe wanted to be a real witch. But when her wish finally comes true, things are not quite what she had imagined. Filled with humor and vitality.

Ahyoka and the Talking Leaves: The Story of the Cherokee Alphabet. By Peter and Connie Roop. Illustrated by Yoshi Miyake. New York: Lothrop, Lee & Shepard, 1992.

> Six-year-old Ahyoka, helps her father, Sequoya of the Cherokee, in developing a complete written language called "talking leaves."

Creepy Cookies. By Tina Vilicich-Solomon. Illustrated by Dianne O'Quinn Burke. New York: Random House, 1996.

> Pleasantly scary collection of over twenty recipes and suggestions for preparing hilariously gruesome goodies. Of course, the recipes are fun and so is the reading!

Daddy and Me. By Jeanne Moutoussamy-Ashe. Photographs by the author. New York: Knopf, 1993.

> A beautiful and touching photo story about tennis player Arthur Ashe and his daughter.

The Down and Up Fall. By Johanna Hurwitz. Illustrated by Gail Owens. New York: Morrow, 1996.

> When Bolivia and her friends Rory and Derek get together,

interesting things always happen, and children enjoy following their adventures.

Family Secrets. By Barbara Corcoran. New York: Atheneum, 1992. Tracy's secure world is shaken when she first learns that she is adopted. A touching, insightful story about the meaning of love, and relationships that are forever.

First Children: Growing Up in the White House. By Katherine Leiner. Portraits by Kathie Keller. New York: Tambourine, 1996.

From Nellie Custis, George Washington's adopted daughter, to Chelsea Clinton, this extraordinary book takes an intimate look at the positives and negatives of growing up in the White House.

Funny Stories. Chosen by Michael Rosen. Illustrated by Tony Blundell. New York: Kingfisher, 1993.

Entertaining collection of zany stories from thirty-nine countries around the world.

King Crow. By Jennifer Armstrong. Illustrated by Eric Rohmann. New York: Crown, 1995.

Set in the time of knights in armor, the beautiful narration and splendid illustrations make this a most enjoyable reading experience.

Lightning Inside You and Other Native American Riddles. Edited by John Bierhorst. Illustrated by Louise Brierley. New York: Morrow, 1992.

Fascinating collection of Native American riddles from North, South, and Central America.

The Phantom Tollbooth. By Norton Juster. Illustrated by Jules Feiffer. New York: Epstein & Carroll, 1961.

For generations children have enjoyed the story about Milo, a somewhat bored youngster, and the day he went through the gates of a large toy toll booth and found himself in the enchanted land beyond!

Pie Magic. By Toby Forward. Illustrated by Laura Cornwell. New York: Tambourine, 1996.

Bertie loves his job as a delivery boy for the best pie bakery in the world. But Bertie has a weight problem, and that makes him sad and lonely—until the day a mysterious stranger comes into the store. Written with keen insight and sensitivity as well as a generous touch of humor.

A Pony for Jeremiah. By Robert H. Miller. Illustrated by Nnaka Bennett. Parsippany, N.J.: Silver Burdett, 1996.
Poignant story about a young African American's coming of age in the mid-1800s.

Puzzle Power! Multidimensional Codes, Illusions, Numbers and Brain Teasers. By David Hawcock. Illustrated by Patrick MacAllister. Boston: Little, Brown, 1994.
Puzzles, pullouts, pop-ups, plus great illustrations make this a perfect book for curious young minds.

Soccer Circus. By Jamie Gilson. Illustrated by Dee deRosa. New York: Lothrop, Lee & Shepard, 1993.
Somehow Hobie Hanson always manages to get himself into a great deal of trouble, but on this trip, a simple overnight soccer tournament, there will be no problem. Or so he promises his dad. So how come he ends up wearing a penguin outfit, rides in a car full of clowns, and does somersaults in gold tights? Very funny reading!

The 13th Floor: A Ghost Story. By Sid Fleischman. Illustrated by Peter Sis. New York: Greenwillow, 1995.
Set in Puritan New England, this entertaining adventure amusingly deals with "triskaidekaphobia," the anxiety some people have about the number 13.

Ages 9 and Up

The Big Bike Race. By Lucy Jane Bledsoe. Illustrated by Sterling Brown. New York: Holiday House, 1995.
Splendid action adventure and sensitive portrayal of a nontraditional family combine to make this a compelling, very readable story.

The Black Stallion's Shadow. By Steven Farley. New York: Random House, 1996.
Strange things have been happening at the horse range, and

Black Stallion has been acting fearful, even of his own shadow. Riveting reading for young fans of the famous horse.

Falcon's Egg. By Luli Gray. Boston: Houghton Mifflin, 1995. Eleven-year-old Falcon finds a strange-looking red egg right in the middle of Central Park and decides to bring it home. But when a dragon hatches from the egg, Falcon needs lots of advice, which is freely given by Great Aunt Emily and a helpful ornithologist. An imaginative adventure, fun to read.

Goosebumps: My Hairiest Adventure. By R.L. Stine. New York: Scholastic, 1994.
"Larry Boyd is the nicest twelve-year-old kid in town!" That's what every one of his friends will say. So how come stray dogs always chase him? And why does he find himself right in the middle of a most chilling adventure—all because he finds an old bottle of "Insta-Tan" in the trash? This book is just an example of the goosebump-giving stories by Stine, a most prolific writer who knows how to make older children into ardent fans as he scares and delights them with his "Reader beware—you're in for a scare!" warning.

In the Path of Lewis and Clark: Traveling the Missouri River. By Peter Lourie. Photographs by the author. Parsippany, N.J.: Silver Burdett, 1997.
In 1804, Lewis and Clark began their historic trek of exploration. In 1995, the author embarked on an identical journey, resulting in this gripping account of the adventure.

Journey to the Heart of Nature: A Guided Exploration. By Joseph Cornell and Michael Deranja. Nevada City, Calif.: Dawn, 1994.
Commissioned by the World Scouts in Geneva, the authors have created a fascinating portrait of the magic and wonders of nature.

Lassie Come Home. By Eric Mowbray Knight. Retold by Rosemary Wells. Illustrated by Susan Jeffers. 1940/New York: Henry Holt, 1995.
Packing an emotional punch, this version of the classic, first published in 1940, preserves all the beauty of the original.

Lost in Merlin's Castle. By P.J. Stray. Parsippany, N.J.: Silver Burdett, 1996.

Spellbinding adventure story about a vacation trip with nothing going as planned, including having to spend a night in a gloomy castle where possible danger awaits. Chills and thrills for mystery fans.

The Most Dangerous Journey: The Life of an African Elephant. By Roger A. Caras. Photographs by the author. New York: Dial, 1995.

Powerful photographs capture the majesty of this fact-filled story about a bull elephant named Ndovu. The author, a well-known naturalist, follows the life cycle of an endangered species and shows the environmental challenges to their existence.

The Mystery of the Sea Dog's Treasure. By P.J. Stray. Parsippany, N.J.: Silver Burdett, 1996.

It all starts with a package filled with mysterious papers and maps. Mark and Kelly, with the help of their science teacher, learn that they may have stumbled onto the long-lost log of Sir Francis Drake, which may lead the finders to a vast treasure Sir Drake was said to have left behind when he visited California in 1579. An engrossing blend of history and suspense.

On Winter's Wind: A Novel. By Patricia Hermes. Boston: Little, Brown, 1995.

The Quaker family that Gen works for is helping slaves escape to Canada, and Gen knows that the reward for revealing this secret to the authorities could be enough to save her own family from a life of poverty. A poignant, powerful story set in the years prior to the Civil War.

Trout Summer. By Jane Leslie Conly. New York: Henry Holt, 1995.

Tender and touching story about twelve-year-old Shana and Cody, her thirteen-year-old sibling, as they try to cope with their parent's divorce.

Ages 10 and Up

Far North. By Will Hobbs. New York: Morrow, 1996.

Gabe, a fifteen-year-old Texan, and his roommate Raymond from a remote Dene Indian village are flying over Canada's Northwest Territories when their small plane goes down in the frozen wilderness. As they struggle to reach safety, an uneasy relationship between these two boys from vastly different cultures changes into an unbreakable bond. A strong tale of suspense and friendship.

Just So Stories. By Rudyard Kipling. Illustrated by Barry Moser. 1912/ New York: Morrow, 1996.

For almost one hundred years, these tales—delightful as well as wise—have entertained young and not-so-young alike. The illustrations add to the magic of this timeless classic.

Nearer Nature. By Jim Arnosky. Illustrated by the author. New York: Lothrop, Lee & Shepard, 1996.

The author, a popular nature writer for children, shares his reflections and observations over the course of a year spent tracking wildlife and tending his Vermont farm. Enhanced by true-to-life black-and-white illustrations.

Talking in Animal. By Terry Farish. New York: Greenwillow, 1996.

Siobhan seems to prefer dogs to people. All Siobhan knows is that for her, communicating with animals comes easier than with humans. But then Siobhan discovers that she and her only human friend, Lester, can talk about cats, dogs, and wolves—and even about love, loss, and courage. A story that speaks gently to young readers.

The Thief. By Megan Whalen Turner. New York: Greenwillow, 1996.

Magus, the king's scholar, has discovered the place where a sacred stone with magic powers can be found. All he needs is an experienced thief to get the treasure for him. He chooses Gen from the king's prison to do the job, but Gen is much smarter and much more trouble than Magus had anticipated. Amusing and original.

Books for Children of All Ages

Circus! Circus! Poems selected by Lee Bennett Hopkins. Illustrated by John O'Brien. New York: Knopf, 1982.

Lion tamers, clowns, acrobats, elephants, and all the other circus people come alive through this collection of sparkling circus poems.

A Jar of Tiny Stars: Poems by NCTE Award-Winning Poets. Edited by Bernice E. Cullinan. Illustrated by Andi Macleod. Portraits by Marc Nadel. Honesdale, Pa.: Wordsong Boyds Mills, 1995.

This lively anthology presents poems by the winners of the National Council of Teachers of English Award for Poetry for Children. All the poems are wonderful, "funny, wise and not the least bit grown up." Kids will love them.

Long Ago in Oregon. By Claudia Lewis. Illustrated by Joel Fontaine. New York: Harper & Row, 1987.

A collection of poems, each a gem, provides a touching look into a world long past.

My Own Song and Other Poems to Groove To. Selected by Michael R. Strickland. Illustrated by Eric Sabee. Honesdale, Pa: Wordsong Boyds Mills, 1997.

Poems that sparkle with music.

Pass It On: African-American Poetry for Children. Selected by Wade Hudson. Illustrated by Floyd Cooper. New York: Scholastic, 1993.

A beautiful collection of African-American poetry that passes on the magic.

Children's Classics

The following is a small sampling of classics in children's literature that should be part of every young child's growing years.

ABC Book. By C.B. Falls. Garden City, N.Y.: Doubleday, 1923. (Ages 2 and up)

Anno's Alphabet. By Mitsumasa Anno. Illustrated by the author. New York: Crowell, 1975. (Ages 2 and up)

Arrow to the Sun: A Pueblo Indian Tale. By Gerald McDermott. Illustrated by the author. New York: Viking, 1974. (Ages 6 and up)

Ben's Trumpet. By Rachel Isadora. Illustrated by the author. New York: Greenwillow, 1979. (Ages 6 and up)

Blueberries for Sal. By Robert McCloskey. Illustrated by the author. New York: Viking, 1948, 1976. (Ages 3 and up)

Brian Wildsmith's ABC. By Brian Wildsmith. Illustrated by the author. Brookfield, Conn.: Millbrook Press, 1962.

Call It Courage. By Armstrong Sperry. Illustrated by the author. New York: Macmillan, 1940, 1968. (Ages 9 and up)

Caps for Sale. By Esphyr Slobodkina. Illustrated by the author. New York: Harper & Row, 1947/New York: Scholastic, 1987. (Ages 3 and up)

The Carrot Seed. By Ruth Krauss. Illustrated by Crockett Johnson. New York: Harper & Row, 1945, 1973. (Ages 2 and up)

Charlotte's Web. By E.B. White. Illustrated by Garth Williams. New York: Harper & Row, 1952, 1980. (Ages 7 and up)

A Christmas Carol. By Charles Dickens. Illustrated by Arthur Rackham. 1843/London: Heineman, 1952. (Ages 5 and up)

Corduroy. By Don Freeman. Illustrated by the author. New York: Viking, 1968. (Ages 3 and up)

Crow Boy. By Taro Yashima. Illustrated by the author. New York: Viking, 1955, 1983. (Ages 5 and up)

Curious George. By H.A. Rey. Illustrated by the author. Boston: Houghton Mifflin, 1941, 1969. (Ages 3 and up)

Freight Train. By Donald Crews. Illustrated by the author. New York: Greenwillow, 1978. (Ages 2 and up)

Frog and Toad Are Friends. By Arnold Lobel. Illustrated by the author. New York: Harper & Row, 1970. (Ages 5 and up)

From the Mixed Up Files of Mrs. Basil E. Frankweiler. By E.L. Konigsburg. Illustrated by the author. New York: Aladdin, 1967. (Ages 9 and up)

Goodnight Moon. By Margaret Wise Brown. Illustrated by Clement Hurd. New York: Harper & Row, 1947, 1975. (Ages 2 and up)

The Happy Lion. By Louise Fatio. Illustrated by Roger Duvoisin. New York: McGraw-Hill, 1954. (Ages 3 and up)

Horton Hatches the Egg. By Dr. Seuss. Illustrated by the author. New York: Random House, 1940, 1968. (Ages 4 and up)

The Island of the Skog. By Steven Kellogg. Illustrated by the author. New York: Dial, 1930, 1973. (Ages 6 and up)

Little House in the Big Woods. By Laura Ingalls Wilder. Illustrated by Garth Williams. New York: Harper and Brothers, 1932, 1987. (Ages 8 and up)

The Little Prince. By Antoine de Saint-Exupery. Translated by Katherine Woods. Illustrated by the author. New York: Harcourt Brace, 1943. (Ages 8 and up)

Little Women. By Louisa May Alcott. Illustrated by Jessie Willcox Smith. Boston: Little, Brown, 1869, 1968. (Ages 10 and up)

Madeline. By Ludwig Bemelmans. Illustrated by the author. New York: Simon & Schuster, 1939/New York: Viking Kestrel, 1987. (Ages 3 and up)

May I Bring a Friend? By Beatrice Schenk deRegniers. Illustrated by Beni Montresor. New York: Atheneum, 1964. (Ages 4 and up)

Mike Mulligan and His Steam Shovel. By Virginia Lee Burton. Illustrated by the author. Boston: Houghton Mifflin, 1939. (Ages 3 and up)

Mr. Gumpy's Outing. By John Burningham. Illustrated by the author. New York: Henry Holt, 1970. (Ages 2 and up)

One Fine Day. By Nonny Hogrogian. Illustrated by the author. New York: Simon & Schuster, 1971. (Ages 5 and up)

One Monday Morning. By Uri Shulevitz. Illustrated by the author. New York: Simon & Schuster, 1967. (Ages 5 and up)

Pat the Bunny. By Dorothy Kunhardt. Illustrated by the author. New York: Golden Books, 1942.

Rosie's Walk. By Pat Hutchins. Illustrated by the author. New York: Macmillan, 1968. (Ages 4 and up)

Sam, Bangs and Moonshine. By Evaline Ness. Illustrated by the author. New York: Henry Holt, 1966. (Ages 6 and up)

Sam Who Never Forgets. By Eve Rice. Illustrated by the author. New York: Greenwillow, 1977. (Ages 2 and up)

The Secret Garden. By Frances Hodgson Burnett. New York: F.A. Stokes, 1911/New York: HarperCollins, 1962. (Ages 5 and up)

The Snowy Day. By Ezra Jack Keats. Illustrated by the author. New York: Viking, 1962. (Ages 3 and up)

Stevie. By John Steptoe. Illustrated by the author. New York: Harper & Row, 1969. (Ages 6 and up)

The Story about Ping. By Marjorie Flack. Illustrated by Kurt Weise. New York: Viking, 1933, 1961. (Ages 3 and up)

The Story of Ferdinand. By Munro Leaf. Illustrated by Robert Lawson. New York: Viking, 1936, 1964. (Ages 4 and up)

Sylvester and the Magic Pebble. By William Steig. Illustrated by the author. New York: Simon & Schuster, 1969. (Ages 6 and up)

The Tale of Peter Rabbit. By Beatrix Potter. Illustrated by the author. London: Warne, 1902, 1987. (Ages 3 and up)

When We Were Very Young. By A.A. Milne. Illustrated by Ernest H. Shepard. New York: Dutton, 1924, 1952. (Ages 3 and up)

Where the Wild Things Are. By Maurice Sendak. Illustrated by the author. New York: Harper & Row, 1963. (Ages 5 and up)

Whose Mouse Are You? By Robert Kraus. Illustrated by Jose Aruego. New York: Macmillan, 1970. (Ages 2 and up)

Winnie the Pooh. By A.A. Milne. Illustrated by Ernest H. Shepard. New York: Dutton, 1926, 1954. (Ages 5 and up)

Wordless Picture Books

Anno's Journey. By Mitsumasa Anno. Illustrated by the author. Cleveland: Collins-World, 1977. (Ages 6 and up)

A wordless journey through town and countryside that holds visual delights.

A Boy, a Dog and a Frog. By Mercer Mayer. Illustrated by the author. New York: Dial, 1967. (Ages 3 and up)

Captivating pen-and-ink drawings encourage young children to supply their own interpretation to the story about a little boy, his dog, and their encounter with a frog. Equally charming wordless books in the series are: *A Boy, a Dog and a Frog and a Friend; Frog* on His Own; Frog Goes to Dinner; and One Frog Too Many.

Bunny Party. By Lena Anderson. Illustrated by the author. New York: Farrar, Straus & Giroux, 1989. (Ages 3 and up)
A child and his little bunny frolic in this wordless book from Sweden.

Do You Want to Be My Friend? By Eric Carle. Illustrated by the author. New York: Harper & Row, 1971. (Ages 3 and up)
Page by page, the illustrations create a cheerful guessing game.

Dressing. By Helen Oxenbury. Illustrated by the author. New York: Wanderer Books, 1981. (Ages 1 and up)
Depicts familiar objects of interest to little ones. The series also includes Playing and Working.

The Grey Lady and the Strawberry Snatcher. By Molly Bang. Illustrated by the author. New York: Four Winds Press, 1980. (Ages 3 and up)
Watch out! The snatcher is trying to take the strawberries from the nice Grey Lady.

Hands Off! By Mario Mariotti. Original Photgraphs by Roberto Marchiori. Brooklyn: Kane-Miller, 1990. (Ages 4 and up)
Lively photographs show a soccer game in action.

The Hunter and the Animals. By Tomie de Paola. Illustrated by the author. New York: Holiday, 1981. (Ages 5 and up)
Kindly animals help a hunter lost in the forest.

Junglewalk. By Nancy Tafuri. Illustrated by the author. New York: Greenwillow, 1988. (Ages 3 and up)
It's bedtime, and a little boy dreams about an adventure with a stately tiger.

Look What I Can Do! By Jose Aruego. Illustrated by the author. New York: Macmillan, 1971. (Ages 5 and up)
Amusing antics between two frisky caribous in this almost wordless book.

Moonlight. By Jan Ormerod. Illustrated by the author. New York: Lothrop, Lee & Shepard, 1982. (Ages 3 and up)
A little girl's going-to-bed ritual is lovingly described in this wordless bedtime story.

Oink. By Arthur Geisert. Illustrated by the author. Boston: Houghton Mifflin, 1991. (Ages 3 and up)

The only word in this funny book is "oink," but the pig family shows that even one word can have a lot of meaning.

Picnic. By Emily Arnold McCully. Illustrated by the author. New York: Harper & Row, 1984. (Ages 4 and up)

A most eventful and exciting picnic for the whole mouse family.

Puss in Boots. Illustrated by John S. Goodall. New York: M.K. McElderry Books/Simon & Schuster 1990. (Ages 6 and up)

Wordless retelling of the charming French fairy tale about a kind cat and the miller's son.

School. By Emily Arnold McCully. Illustrated by the author. New York: Harper & Row, 1987. (Ages 3 and up)

A curious little mouse decides to follow her siblings to school to find out what school is all about.

Surprise Picnic. By John S. Goodall. Illustrated by the author. New York: Atheneum, 1977. (Ages 3 and up)

A cat and two little kittens go on a picnic and find lots of fun and adventure.

Truck. By Donald Crews. Illustrated by the author. New York: Greenwillow, 1980. (Ages 6 and up)

Bold and colorful illustrations trace a truck from the loading dock to its San Francisco destination in this very "readable" wordless book.

We Hide, You Seek. By Jose Aruego and Ariane Dewey. Illustrated by Jose Aruego. New York: Greenwillow, 1979. (Ages 5 and up)

Amusing illustrations show a lively game of hide-and-seek.

Chapter Books

Arthur's Funny Money. By Lillian Hoban. Illustrated by the author. New York: Harper & Row, 1981. (Ages 4 and up)

Violet is having trouble with her math problems, and big brother Arthur is no help at all. Warm and funny.

Blast Off! Poems about Space. Selected by Lee Bennett Hopkins. Illustrated by Melissa Sweet. New York: HarperCollins, 1995. (Ages 4 and up)

> Soar into space with this collection of lovely poems that celebrate the celestial skies.

Busy Buzzing Bumblebees and Other Tongue Twisters. By Alvin Schwartz. Illustrated by Paul Meisel. New York: HarperCollins, 1992. (Ages 4 and up)

> A collection of tongue twisters.

The Case of the Two Masked Robbers. By Lillian Hoban. Illustrated by the author. New York: Harper & Row, 1986. (Ages 5 and up)

> Who has stolen Mrs. Turtle's eggs from the Meadow Marsh Bank? A mystery tale just right to keep young readers engaged to the clever end.

Commander Toad and the Planet of the Grapes. By Jane Yolen. Illustrated by the author. New York: Coward, McCann & Geoghegan, 1982. (Ages 6 and up)

> While traveling "across the galaxy from star to star" Commander Toad and his crew land on a most mysterious planet.

Danny and the Dinosaur. By Syd Hoff. Illustrated by the author. New York: HarperCollins, 1958, 1986. (Ages 4 and up)

> In this sparkling story in chapters, Danny visits the museum and makes friends with a huge but very amiable dinosaur.

Days with Frog and Toad. By Arnold Lobel. Illustrated by the author. New York: Harper & Row, 1979.

> Children enjoy reading stories from the Frog and Toad series. In this story two friends like to spend time together but find that sometimes it's nice to be alone.

The Friends of Abu Ali: Three More Tales of the Middle East. Retold by Dorothy O. Van Woerkom. Illustrated by Harold Berson. New York: Macmillan, 1978. (Ages 4 and up)

> In this humorous sequel to *Abu Ali,* the further misadventures of the endearing but not too clever Abu Ali and his friends are retold.

Henry and Mudge and the Long Weekend. By Cynthia Rylant. Illustrated by Sucie Stevenson. New York: Bradbury, 1992. (Ages 4 and up)

It's raining outside, and Henry and his dog, Mudge, are bored, with nothing to do. That is, until Henry's mother has a great idea!

Marigold and Grandma on the Town. By Stephanie Calmenson. Illustrated by Mary Chalmers. New York: HarperCollins, 1994. (Ages 4 and up)

Marigold and her grandmother, two charming bunnies, spend a wonderful day together.

Mouse Soup. By Arnold Lobel. Illustrated by the author. New York: Harper & Row, 1977. (Ages 4 and up)

A tale about a clever little mouse and a very hungry weasel.

Nate the Great and the Fishy Prize. By Marjorie Weinman Sharmat. Illustrated by Marc Simont. New York: Coward-McCann, 1985. (Ages 4 and up)

Nate, the great detective, has a very strange case to solve. A prize he had hoped his dog would win is missing, and there is something very fishy about it!

Wagon Wheels. By Barbara Brenner. Illustrated by Don Bolognese. New York: Harper & Row, 1978. (Ages 4 and up)

A realistic, touching story about a pioneer family facing their first, harsh winter in far-from-home Kansas, and the Osage Indians who saved them from starvation.

Children's Circle Home Video Library Titles Based on Picture Books

Below is a sample selection from the Children's Circle Home Video Library. All are recommended for family viewing.

The Maurice Sendak Library

This special edition includes Sendak's most beloved stories for children on video. In a brief documentary segment at the end, Sendak provides a fascinating glimpse into the world of his art. Included are:

- *Alligators All Around*
- *One Was Johnny*
- *Pierre*
- *Chicken Soup with Rice*

- *Where the Wild Things Are*
- *In the Night Kitchen*
- *Getting to Know Maurice Sendak*

The Ezra Jack Keats Library
This charming collection of Keats's stories about Peter and his friends also features a short documentary introducing the artist. Included in this collector's edition are:

- *The Snowy Day*
- *Whistle for Willie*
- *Peter's Chair*
- *A Letter to Amy*
- *Pet Show!*
- *The Trip*
- *Getting to Know Ezra Jack Keats*

Stories from the Black Tradition
An award-winning video featuring folk and fairy tales from Africa:

- *Why Mosquitoes Buzz in People's Ears*, retold by Verna Aardema; illustrated by Leo and Diane Dillon
- *Mufaro's Beautiful Daughters*, by John Steptoe
- *A Story—A Story*, by Gail E. Hailey
- *The Village of Round and Square Houses*, by Ann Grifalconi

The Snowman
This nonverbal winter tale by Raymond Briggs about a boy and his snowman is rendered in muted pastel and coupled with an exquisite orchestral score, making it a treat for all seasons.

Maurice Sendak's Really Rosie
This film is based on characters from Maurice Sendak's *The Nutshell Library* and *The Sign on Rosie's Door*. Music is composed and sung by Carole King. Convinced of her limitless talent, charms, and ability, Rosie sweeps the neighborhood Nutshell Kids into the beam of her private spotlight as they perform in her pretend movie.

Harold and the Purple Crayon and Other Harold Stories
When the ingenious artist Harold brandishes his purple crayon, three exciting adventures appear—or disappear!

The William Steig Library
At last, four stellar Steig stories are together in one volume, along with a chat with the celebrated *New Yorker* cartoonist.

- *The Amazing Bone*
- *Doctor De Soto*
- *Brave Irene*
- *Sylvester and the Magic Pebble*
- *Getting to Know William Steig*

Stories from the Jewish Tradition
Two enchanting Hanukkah stories to share with children of all ages.

- *In the Month of Kislev,* by Nina Jaffe; illustrated by Louise August
- *Zlateh the Goat,* by Isaac Bashevis Singer

Strega Nonna and Other Stories
Children explore the cultures of four continents in these delightful tales.

- *Strega Nonna,* by Tomi de Paola
- *Tikki Tikki Tembo,* by Arlene Mosel; illustrated by Blair Lent
- *The Foolish Frog,* by Pete and Charles Seeger; illustrated by Miloslav Jagr

Christmas Stories
Charming stories that bring the Christmas tradition to life for children of all ages.

- *Morris's Disappearing Bag,* by Rosemary Wells
- *The Clown of God,* by Tomi de Paola
- *The Little Drummer Boy,* by Katherine Davis, Henry Onorati, and Harry Simeone; illustrated by Ezra Jack Keats
- *Max's Christmas,* by Rosemary Wells

Interactive Children's Literature
Nonfiction

The Way Things Work by David Macaulay
My First Incredible Amazing Dictionary by Dorling Kindersley

Dorling Kindersley Multimedia
Houghton Mifflin
95 Madison Avenue
New York, NY 10016

This multimedia series of nonfiction reference books offers children a new way of exploring science and technology concepts and the meanings of words. With a click of a mouse, each word, scientific principle, and invention is explained and illustrated in amazing detail. These resource books combine fascinating animations and sounds, as they lead children down an educational path of new discoveries.

Fiction

Titles from the Living Books series:

Arthur's Birthday by Marc Brown
Arthur's Teacher Trouble by Marc Brown
The Berenstain Bears Get Stage Fright by Stan and Jan Berenstain
Green Eggs and Ham by Dr. Seuss
Just Me and My Dad by Mercer Mayer
Aesop's Fables: The Tortoise and the Hare

Living Books
Broderbund Software, Inc.
500 Redwood Blvd.
Novato, Ca. 94948

Living Books are multimedia versions of original storybooks written by well-known children's authors. Their beautiful illustrations and unique use of sound and music keep children engaged for hours. Clicking on pictures causes actions to occur that add detail to the stories. This program provides a wonderful way to develop reading skills. These stories can be experienced by children in English, Spanish, or Japanese. Children will truly enjoy and learn from these programs.

Titles from the Discis Books series:

Tales of Benjamin Bunny by Beatrix Potter
Cinderella
The Tale of Peter Rabbit by Beatrix Potter

Discis Books: Discis Knowledge Research, Inc.
NYCCPO Box #45099
Toronto, Ontario, Canada M2N 6NZ

> Discis Books provide a wonderful way for children to develop word recognition, vocabulary, and reading comprehension skills. The illustrations are duplicates of the original storybook versions. Children can interact by clicking on pictures and words for definitions and pronunciations. These interactive storybooks are also provided in Spanish, French, and Cantonese.

Children's Book Awards

Publication dates for awards books are usually the year of or year before the award.

Jane Addams Children's Book Award

Jane Addams Peace Association
Awarded to children's narrative and picture books that promote the cause of peace, social justice, world community, and gender and racial equality.

1996
The Well: David's Story. By Mildred D. Taylor. (Dial)

Special Commendation 1996
Middle Passage: White Ships/Black Cargo. By Tom Feelings. (Dial)

1997
Growing Up in Coal Country. By Susan Campbell. (Houghton Mifflin)

Picture Book Award 1997
Wilma Unlimited: How Wilma Rudolph Became the Fastest Woman in the World. By Katherine Krull. Illustrated by David Diaz. (Harcourt Brace Jovanovich)

Irma S. and James H. Black Award
Bank Street College of Education
Award given each spring to a book for young children. Selects books for excellence in text and illustrations.

1995
Wicked Jack. By Connie Nordhielm Woolridge. Illustrated by Will Hillenbrand. (Holiday House)

1996
Jojofu. Michael P. Waite. Illustrated by Yoriko Ito. (Lothrop, Lee & Shepard)

Boston Globe–Horn Book Awards*
Presented annually by the *Boston Globe* and *The Horn Book Magazine.* Through 1975, two awards were given, one for outstanding text and one for outstanding illustration; in 1976 the award categories were changed and currently are outstanding fiction or poetry, outstanding nonfiction, and outstanding illustration.

1967
Text: *The Little Fishes.* By Erik Christian Haugaard. (Houghton Mifflin)
Illustration: *London Bridge Is Falling Down!* By Peter Spier. (Doubleday)

1968
Text: *The Spring River.* By John Lawson. (HarperCollins)
Illustration: *Tikki Tikki Tembo.* By Arlene Mosel. Illustrated by Blair Lent. (Henry Holt)

1969
Text: *A Wizard of Earthsea.* By Ursula K. LeGuin. (Houghton Mifflin, Parnassus)
Illustration: *The Adventures of Paddy Pork.* By John S. Goodall. (Harcourt Brace)

1970
Text: *The Intruder.* By John Rowe Townsend. (HarperCollins)
Illustration: *Hi, Cat!* By Ezra Jack Keats. (Macmillan)

---

*Some of the above material is from *Literature and the Child.* Third Edition. By Bernice E. Cullinan and Lee Galda. New York: Harcourt Brace Jovanovich, 1994.

1971
Text: *A Room Made of Windows.* By Eleanor Cameron. (Little, Brown/
Atlantic)
Illustration: *If I Built a Village.* By Kazue Mizumura. (HarperCollins)

1972
Text: *Tristan and Iseult.* By Rosemary Sutcliff. (Dutton)
Illustration: *Mr. Gumpy's Outing.* By John Burningham. (Henry Holt)

1973
Text: *The Dark Is Rising.* By Susan Cooper. (Atheneum/McElderry)
Illustration: *King Stork.* By Trina Schart Hyman. (Little, Brown)

1974
Text: *M.C. Higgins, the Great.* By Virginia Hamilton. (Macmillan)
Illustration: *Jambo Means Hello.* By Muriel Feelings. Illustrated by
Tom Feelings. (Dial)

1975
Text: *Transport 7–41-R.* By T. Degens. (Viking)
Illustration: *Anno's Alphabet.* By Mitsumasa Anno. (HarperCollins)

1976
Fiction: *Unleaving.* By Jill Paton Walsh. (Farrar, Straus & Giroux)
Illustration: *Thirteen.* By Remy Charlip and Jerry Joyner. (Four Winds)

1977
Fiction: *Child of the Owl.* By Lawrence Yep. (HarperCollins)
Illustration: *Granfa' Grig Had a Pig and Other Rhymes without Rea-
son from Mother Goose.* By Wallace Tripp. (Little, Brown)

1978
Fiction: *The Westing Game.* By Ellen Raskin. (Dutton)
Illustration: *Anno's Journey.* By Mitsumasa Anno. (Philomel)

1979
Fiction: *Humbug Mountain.* By Sid Fleischman. (Little, Brown)
Illustration: *The Snowman.* By Raymond Briggs. (Random House)

1980
Fiction: *Conrad's War.* By Andrew Davies. (Crown)
Illustration: *The Garden of Andrew Gasazi.* By Chris Van Allsburg.
(Houghton Mifflin)

1981

Text: *The Leaving.* By Lynn Hall. (Scribner)
Illustration: *Outside Over There.* By Maurice Sendak. (HarperCollins)

1982

Fiction: *Playing Beatie Bow.* By Ruth Park. (Atheneum)
Illustration: *A Visit to William Blake's Inn: Poems for Innocent and Experienced Travelers.* By Nancy Williard. Illustrated by Alice and Martin Provensen. (Harcourt Brace Jovanovich)

1983

Fiction: *Sweet Whisper, Brother Rush.* By Virginia Hamilton. (Philomel)
Illustration: *A Chair for My Mother.* By Vera B. Williams. (Greenwillow)

1984

Fiction: *A Little Fear.* By Patricia Wrightson. (Atheneum)
Illustration: *Jonah and the Great Fish.* Retold and Illustrated by Warwick Hutton. (McElderry)

1985

Fiction: *The Moves Make the Man.* By Bruce Brooks. (Harper-Collins)
Illustration: *Mama Don't Allow.* By Thacher Hurd. (Harper-Collins)
Special Award: *1,2,3.* By Tana Hoban. (Greenwillow)

1986

Fiction: *In Summer Light.* By Zibby Oneal. (Viking)
Illustration: *The Paper Crane.* By Molly Bang. (Greenwillow)

1987

Fiction: *Rabble Starkey.* By Lois Lowry. (Houghton Mifflin)
Illustration: *Mufaro's Beautiful Daughters.* By John Steptoe. (Lothrop, Lee & Shepard)

1988

Fiction: *The Friendship.* By Mildred Taylor. (Dial)
Illustration: *Boy of the Three-Year Nap.* By Diane Synder. Illustrated by Allen Say. (Houghton Mifflin)

1989
Fiction: *The Village by the Sea.* By Paula Fox. (Orchard)
Illustration: *Shy Charles.* By Rosemary Wells. (Dial)

1990
Fiction: *Maniac Magee.* By Jerry Spinelli. (Little, Brown)
Illustration: *Lon Po Po.* Translated and Illustrated by Ed Young. (Philomel)
Special Award: *Valentine and Orson.* By Nancy Ekholm Burkert. (Farrar, Straus & Giroux)

1991
Fiction: *The True Confessions of Charlotte Doyle.* By Avi. (Orchard)
Illustration: *The Tale of the Mandarin Ducks.* By Katherine Peterson. Illustrated by Leo and Diane Dillon. (Lodestar)

1992
Fiction: *Missing May.* By Cynthia Rylan. (Orchard)
Picture Book: *Seven Blind Mice.* By Ed Young. (Philomel)

1993
Fiction: *Ajeemah and His Son.* By James Berry. (HarperCollins)
Picture Book: *The Fortune Tellers.* By Loyd Alexander. Illustrated by Trina Schart Hyman. (Dutton)

1994
Fiction: *Scooter.* By Very Williams. (Greenwillow)
Picture Book: *Grandfather's Journey.* By Allen Say. (Houghton Mifflin)

1995
Fiction: *Some of the Kinder Planets.* By Tim Wynne-Jones. (Orchard/ Kroupa)
Picture Book: *John Henry.* Retold by Julius Lester. Illustrated by Jerry Pinkney. (Dial)

1996
Fiction: *Poppy.* By Avi. Illustrated by Brian Floca. (Orchard)
Picture Book: *In the Rain with Baby Duck.* By Amy Hest. Illustrated by Jill Barton. (Candlewick)

Randolph Caldecott Medal*

The Caldecott Medal, named in honor of the nineteenth-century illustrator, has been awarded annually since 1938, to the illustrator of the most distinguished picture book for children published in the United States during the preceding year. Where no separate illustrator is listed, the author is the illustrator.

1960
Nine Days to Christmas. By Marie Hall Ets and Aurora Labastida. Illustrated by Marie Hall Ets. (Viking)

1961
Baboushka and the Three Kings. By Ruth Robbins. Illustrated by Nicolas Sidjakov. (Parnassus)

1962
Once a Mouse . . . By Marica Brown. (Scribner)

1963
The Snowy Day. By Ezra Jack Keats. (Viking)

1964
Where the Wild Things Are. By Maurice Sendak. (Harper & Row)

1965
May I Bring a Friend? By Beatrice Schenk de Regniers. Illustrated by Beni Montresor. (Atheneum)

1966
Always Room for One More. By Sorche Nic Leodhas. Illustrated by Nonny Hogrogian. (Henry Holt)

1967
Sam, Bangs and Moonshine. By Evaline Ness. (Henry Holt)

1968
Drummer Hoff. By Barbara Emberley. Illustrated by Ed Emberley. (Prentice-Hall)

---

*Some of the above material is from *Children's Book Awards and Prizes.* By the Children's Book Council. New York: Children's Book Council, 1992.

1969
The Fool of the World and the Flying Ship. Retold by Arthur Ransome. Illustrated by Uri Shulevitz. (Farrar, Straus & Giroux)

1970
Sylvester and the Magic Pebble. By William Steig. (Windmill/Simon & Schuster)

1971
A Story—A Story. By Gail E. Haley. (Atheneum)

1972
One Fine Day. By Nonny Hogrogian. (Macmillan)

1973
The Funny Little Woman. Retold by Arlene Mosel. Illustrated by Blair Lent. (Dutton)

1974
Duffy and the Devil. Retold by Harve Zemach. Illustrated by Margot Zemach. (Farrar, Straus & Giroux)

1975
Arrow to the Sun. By Gerald McDermott. (Viking)

1976
Why Mosquitoes Buzz in People's Ears. Retold by Verna Aardema. Illustrated by Leo and Diane Dillon. (Dial)

1977
Ashanti to Zulu: African Traditions. By Margaret Musgrove. Illustrated by Leo and Diane Dillon. (Dial)

1978
Noah's Ark. By Jacob Revius. Illustrated by Peter Spier. (Doubleday)

1979
The Girl Who Loved Wild Horses. By Paul Goble. (Bradbury)

1980
Ox-Cart Man. By Donald Hall. Illustrated by Barbara Cooney. (Viking)

1981
The Fables. By Arnold Lobel. (Harper & Row)

1982
Jumanji. By Chris Van Allsburg. (Houghton Mifflin)

1983
Shadow. By Blaise Cendrars. Illustrated by Marcia Brown. (Scribner)

1984
The Glorious Flight: Across the Channel with Louis Bleriot. By Alice and Martin Provensen. (Viking)

1985
Saint George and the Dragon. Retold by Margaret Hodges. Illustrated by Trina Schart Hyman. (Little, Brown)

1986
The Polar Express. By Chris Van Allsburg. (Houghton Mifflin)

1987
Hey, Al. By Arthur Yorinks. Illustrated by Richard Egielski. (Farrar, Straus & Giroux)

1988
Owl Moon. By Jane Yolen. Illustrated by John Schoenherr. (Philomel)

1989
Song and Dance Man. By Karen Ackerman. Illustrated by Stephen Gammell. (Knopf)

1990
Lon Po Po: A Red-Riding Hood Story from China. Translated and Illustated by Ed Young. (Philomel)

1991
Black and White. By David Macaulay (Houghton Mifflin)

1992
Tuesday. By David Wiesner. (Clarion)

1993
Mirette on the High Wire. By Emily Arnold McCully. (Putnam)

1994
Grandfather's Journey. By Allen Say. (Houghton Mifflin)

1995
Smoky Night. By Eve Bunting. Illustrated by David Diaz. (Harcourt Brace Jovanovich)

1996
Officer Buckle and Gloria. Peggy Rathmann. (Putnam)

1997
Golem. David Wiesniewski. (Clarion)

Coretta Scott King Awards
These awards recognize annually an outstanding African-American author and illustrator.

1970
Text: *Martin Luther King, Jr.: Man of Peace.* By Lillie Patterson. (Garrard)

1971
Text: *Black Troubador: Langston Hughes.* By Charlemae Rollins. (Rand McNally)

1972
Text: *Seventeen Black Artists.* By Elton C. Fax. (Dodd)

1973
Text: *I Never Had It Made.* By Jackie Robinson as told to Alfred Duckett. (Putnam)

1974
Award for Text and Illustration: *Ray Charles.* By Sharon Bell Mathis. Illustrated by George Ford. (HarperCollins)

1975
Text: *The Legend of Africana.* By Dorothy Robinson. Illustrated by Herbert Temple. (Johnson)

1976
Text: *Duey's Tale.* By Pearl Bailey. (Harcourt Brace Jovanovich)

1977

Text: *The Story of Stevie Wonder.* By James Haskins. (Lothrop, Lee & Shepard)

1978

Award for Text and Illustration: *Africa Dream.* By Eloise Greenfield. Illustration by Carole Byard. (HarperCollins)

1979

Text: *Escape to Freedom.* By Ossie Davis. (Viking)

Illustration: *Something on My Mind.* By Nikki Grimes. Illustrated by Tom Feelings. (Dial)

1980

Text: *The Young Landlords.* By Walter Dean Myers. (Viking)

Illustration: *Cornrows.* By Camille Yarbrough. Illustrated by Carole Byard. (Coward)

1981

Text: *This Life.* By Sidney Poitier. (Knopf)

Illustration: *Beat the Story Drum: Pum, Pum.* By Ashley Bryan. (Atheneum)

1982

Text: *Let the Circle Be Unbroken.* By Mildred D. Taylor. (Dial)

Illustration: *Mother Crocodile: An Uncle Amadou Tale from Senegal.* Adapted by Rosa Guy. Illustrated by John Steptoe. (Delacorte)

1983

Text: *Sweet Whispers, Brother Rush.* By Virginia Hamilton. (Philomel)

Illustration: *Black Child.* By Peter Magubane. (Knopf)

1984

Text: *Everett Anderson's Good-Bye.* By Lucille Clifton. Illustrated by Ann Grifalconi. (Holt, Rinehart and Winston)

Illustration: *My Mama Needs Me.* By Mildred Pitts Walter. Illustrated by Pat Cummings. (Lothrop, Lee & Shepard)

1985

Text: *Motown and Didi.* By Walter Dean Myers. (Viking)

1986
Text: *The People Could Fly: American Black Folktales.* By Virginia Hamilton. Illustrated by Leo and Diane Dillon. (Knopf)
Illustration: *Patchwork Quilt.* By Valerie Flournoy. Illustrated by Jerry Pinkney. (Dial)

1987
Text: *Justin and the Best Biscuits in the World.* By Mildred Pitts Walter. Illustrated by Catherine Stock. (Lothrop, Lee & Shepard)
Illustration: *Half a Moon and One Whole Star.* By Crecent Dragonwagon. Illustrated by Jerry Pinkney. (Macmillan)

1988
Text: *The Friendship.* By Mildred D. Taylor. Illustrated by Max Ginsburg. (Dial)
Illustration: *Mufaro's Beautiful Daughters: An African Tale.* By John Steptoe. (Lothrop, Lee & Shepard)

1989
Text: *Fallen Angels.* By Walter Dean Myers. (Scholastic)
Illustration: *Mirandy and Brother Wind.* By Patricia McKissack. Illustrated by Jerry Pinkney. (Knopf)

1990
Text: *A Long Hard Journey: The Story of the Pullman Porter.* By Patricia and Frederick McKissack. (Walker)
Illustration: *Nathaniel Talking.* By Eloise Greenfield. Illustrated by Jan Spivey Gilchrist. (Black Butterfly)

1991
Text: *The Road to Memphis.* By Mildred D. Taylor. (Dial)
Illustration: *Aida.* By Leontyne Price. Illustrated by Leo and Diane Dillon. (Gulliver/Harcourt Brace Jovanovich)

1992
Text: *Now Is Your Time! The African-American Struggle for Freedom.* By Walter Dean Myers. (HarperCollins)
Illustration: *Tar Beach.* By Faith Ringgold. (Crown)

1993
Text: *The Dark-Thirty: Southern Tales of the Supernatural.* By Patricia C. McKissack. Illustrated by Brian Pinkney. (Knopf)

Illustration: *The Origin of Life on Earth: An African Creation Myth.* By David A. Anderson. Illustrated by Kathleen Atkins Wilson. (Sight Productions)

1994

Text: *Toning the Sweep.* By Angela Johnson. (Orchard)
Illustration: *Soul Looks Back in Wonder.* Poems by Maya Angelou, et al. Illustrated by Tom Feelings. (Dial)

1995

Text: *Christmas in the Big House, Christmas in the Quarters.* By Patricia C. and Fredrick L. McKissack. Illustrated by John Thompson. (Scholastic)
Illustration: *The Creation.* By James Weldon Johnson. Illustrated by James Ransome. (Holiday)

1996

Text: *Her Stories.* By Virginia Hamilton. Illustrated by Leo and Diane Dillon. (Blue Sky)
Illustration: *The Middle Passage: White Ships/Black Cargo.* Introduction by Dr. John Henrik Clarke. Illustrated by Tom Feelings. (Dial)

1997

Text: *SLAM!* By Walter Dean Meyers. (Scholastic)
Illustration: *Minty: A Story of Young Harriet Tubman.* By Alan Schroeder. Illustrated by Jerry Pinkney. (Dial)

Ezra Jack Keats New Writer Award

This award is given to a promising new writer of picture books for children, ages nine and under, whose work reflects the tradition of Ezra Jack Keats. The winning book should portray the universal qualities of childhood, strong supportive family and adult relationships, and the multicultural nature of our planet. The author should not have published more than six books. Entries are judged on outstanding features of the text. However, the quality of the illustrations plays an important part in the decision of the judges. Candidates need not be both author and illustrator. A cash award of $1,000 coupled with the prestigious Ezra Jack Keats medallion, inscribed with the recipient's name, is presented to the winning author at a reception, at The New York Public Library Early Childhood Resource and Information Center. For more information, please write to the program coordinator, Hannah Nuba, The New York Public Library Early Childhood Resource and Information Center, 66 Leroy Street, New York, NY 10014.

1986
The Patchwork Quilt. By Valerie Flournoy. Illustrated by Jerry Pinkney. (Dial)

1987
Jamaica's Find. By Juanita Havill. Illustrated by Anne Sibley O'Brien. (Houghton Mifflin)

1989
Anna's Special Present. By Yoriko Tsutsui. Illustrated by Akiko Hayashi. (Viking)

1991
Tell Me a Story Mama. By Angela Johnson. Illustrated by David Soman. (Orchard)

1993
Tar Beach. By Faith Ringgold (Little, Brown)

1995
Taxi! Taxi! By Cari Best. Illustrated by Dale Gottlieb. (Little, Brown)

1997
Calling the Doves. By Juan Felipe Herrera. Illustrated by Elly Simmons. (Children's Book Press)

International Reading Association Children's Book Award
This award is presented annually for a children's book by an author of unusual promise. The following list gives titles of winners since the inception of the award. Since 1987, the award has been presented for both picture books and novels.

1975
Transport 7–41-R. By T. Degens. (Viking)

1976
Dragonwings. By Lawrence Yep. (Harper & Row)

1977
A String in the Harp. By Nancy Bond. Illustrated by Allen Davis. (Atheneum)

1978
A Summer to Die. By Lois Lowry. Illustrated by Jenni Oliver. (Houghton Mifflin)

1979
Reserved for Mark Anthony Crowder. By Alison Smith. (Dutton)

1980
Words by Heart. By Ouida Sebestyen. (Little, Brown)

1981
My Own Private Sky. By Delores Beckman. (Dutton)

1982
Goodnight Mr. Tom. By Michelle Magorian. (Kestral/HarperCollins)

1983
The Dark-angel. By Meredith Ann Pierce. (Little, Brown)

1984
Ratha's Creature. By Clare Bell. (Atheneum)

1985
Badger on the Barge and Other Stories. By Janni Howker. (MacRae/ HarperCollins)

1986
Prairie Songs. By Pam Conrad. Illustrated by Darryl S. Zudeck. (HarperCollins)

1987
Younger Reader: *The Line Up Book.* By Marisabina Russo. (Greenwillow)
Older Reader: *After the Dancing Days.* By Margaret I. Rostowski. (HarperCollins)

1988
Younger Reader : *The Third-Story Cat.* By Leslie Baker. (Little, Brown)
Older Reader: *The Ruby in the Smoke.* By Philip Pullman. (Knopf)

1989
Younger Reader: *Rechenka's Eggs.* By Patricia Polacco. (Philomel)
Older Reader: *Probably Still Nick Swansen.* By Virginia Euwer Wolff.
(Henry Holt)

1990
Younger Reader: *No Star Nights.* By Anna Egan Smucker. Illustrated
by Steve Johnson. (Knopf)
Older Reader: *Children of the River.* By Linda Crew. (Delacorte)

1991
Younger Reader: *Is This a House for the Hermit Crab?* By Megan
McDonald. Illustrated by S.D. Schindler. (Orchard)
Older Reader: *Under the Hawthorne Tree.* By Marita Conlon-
McKenna. Illustrated by Donald Teskey. (O'Brien Press)

1992
Younger Reader: *Ten Little Rabbits.* By Virginia Grossman. Illustrated
by Sylvia Long. (Chronicle)
Older Reader: *Rescue Josh McGuire.* By Ben Mikaelsen. (Hyperion)

1993
Younger Reader: *Old Turtle.* By Douglas Wood. (Pfeifer-Hamilton)
Older Reader: *Letters from Rifka.* By Karen Hesse. (Henry Holt)

1994
Younger Reader: *Sweet Clara and the Freedom Quilt.* By Debra
Hopkinson. Illustrated by James Ransome. (Random House)
Older Reader: *Behind the Secret Window.* By Nellie S. Toll. (Dutton)

1995
Younger Reader: *The Ledgerbook of Thomas Blue Eagle.* By Jewel H.
Grutman, Gay Matthaei, and Adam Civjanovi. (Thomasson-Grant)
Older Reader: *Spite Fences.* By Trudy Krisher. (Delacorte)
Informational Reader: *Stranded at Plymouth Plantation 1626.* By Gary
Bowen. (HarperCollins)

1996
Younger Reader: *More About Anything Else.* By Mary Bradey and
Chris Soentpiet. (Orchard)
Older Reader: *The King's Shadow.* By Elizabeth Alder. (Farrar, Straus
& Giroux)

Informational Reader: *The Case of the Mummified Pig and Other Mystery in Nature.* By Susan E. Quinland. (Boyds Mills)

1997

Younger Reader: *Fabulous Flying Fandinis.* By Ingrid Slyder. (Cobblehill/Dutton)

Older Reader: *Don't You Dare Read This, Mrs. Dunphrey.* By Margaret Paterson Haddix. (Simon & Schuster)

Informational Reader: *The Brooklyn Bridge.* By Elizabeth Mann. Illustrated by Alan Witschonke. (Mikaya Press)

Magazines for Children

American Girl (Girls ages 8–12)

Features step-by-step arts and craft ideas, interesting short stories, puzzles, homework helpers, school fashion ideas, recipes, etc. Also includes fascinating paper dolls of real American girls in history.

To order:

American Girl

P.O. Box 420210

Palm Coast, FL 32142

800–234–1278

Babybug (Ages 6 months–2 years)

A delightful listening and looking magazine for infants and toddlers.

To order:

Carus Publishing

P.O. Box 503

Mt. Morris, IL 61054

800–827–0227

Chickadee (Ages 3–9)

Easy-to-read stories, puzzles, science experiments, etc., all designed to teach and entertain.

To order:

Young Naturalist Foundation

225 Arrow Avenue

Buffalo, NY 14207

416-868–6001

Child Life (Ages 7–9)
The focus is on introducing young children to a healthy lifestyle
through articles on nutrition, exercise, and healthful living. Also fea-
tures information about other cultures and the beauty of nature.
To order:
Children's Better Health Institute
P.O. Box 7133
Red Oak, IA 51591
515–280–3739

Children's Playmate (Ages 6–8)
Interesting fiction and nonfiction stories for beginning readers, includ-
ing easy recipes, book reviews, cartoons, and good health guidelines.
To order:
Children's Better Health Institute
P.O. Box 7133
Red Oak, IA 51591
515–280–3739

Crayola Kids Magazine (Ages 3–8)
Perfect introduction for young children to the pleasure of reading.
To order:
Meredeth Publishing Service
Customer Service
P.O. Box 400425
Des Moines, IA 50340
800–846–7968

Cricket (Ages 7–14)
Features activities and stories for children from all over the world,
designed to inspire a love for books and reading.
To order:
Carus Publishing
P.O. Box 593
Mt. Morris, IL 61054
800–827–0227

Disney Adventures (Ages 6–14)
Covers sports, entertainment, sciences, travel, comics, puzzles, etc.
Focus is on reading for entertainment.

To order:
Disney Adventures
P.O. Box 420235
Palm Coast, FL 32142
800–829–5146

Dolphin Log (Ages 7–15)
Appears bimonthly, published by the Cousteau Society. Featured
are nonfiction articles about science, marine biology, and global environment.
To order:
The Cousteau Society
870 Greenbrier Circle, Suite 402
Chesapeake, VA 23320
757–523–9335

Faces (Ages 8–14)
Connected with the Anthropology Department of the American
Museum of Natural History, this magazine introduces children to
the customs among people around the world while encouraging
respect for the varied lifestyles and beliefs found throughout the
world.
To order:
Cobblestone Publishing Co.
7 School Street
Petersborough, NH 03458
603–924–7209

Fantastic Flyer Magazine (Ages 2–12)
Published by Delta Airlines and distributed free to young passengers
on Delta flights (and homes), this frank marketing idea fosters knowledge of geography and love of travel. Articles explore the different
customs around the world, emphasizing that children who live dif-
ferently share many of the same interests with all other children
around the globe.

Happy Times (Ages 3–5)
Bible lessons for the very young through stories, poems, puzzles,
and songs.

To order:
Concordia Publishing House
35–58 S. Jefferson Avenue
St. Louis, MO 63118
314–268–1000

Highlights for Children (Ages 2–12)
"Fun with a Purpose" is the focus of this magazine. Each issue features stories, poems, arts and crafts and science activities, as well as riddles and jokes and suggestions about handling personal problems.
To order:
Highlights for Children, Inc.
P.O. Box 262
Columbus, OH 43272–0002
800–848–8922

HIP (Ages 8–14)
Beginning publication in January 1995, this bimonthly magazine focuses on hearing-impaired children. Offers wide range of materials, including profiles of special people who can serve as role models, and columns on advice, technology, and communication. Includes games and puzzles. Available by subscription only.
To order:
HIP
1563 Solano Avenue
Berkeley, CA 94707
510–527–8993

Hopscotch: The Magazine for Young Girls (Ages 6–12)
The aim is to encourage and challenge young girls to enjoy their young years, while they make the most of the opportunities that surround them.
To order:
Bluffton News Publishing Co.
P.O. Box 164
Bluffton, OH 45817–0164
419–358–4610

Humpty Dumpty Magazine (Ages 4–6)

Emphasis is on health through stories, poems, activities, puzzles, crafts, and nutritious recipes for the very young.

To order:

Children's Better Health Institute

P.O. Box 7133

Red Oak, IA 51591

515–280–3739

Jack and Jill (Ages 7–10)

This general interest magazine concentrates on fitness, health, and nutrition. At the same time, the articles, poems, comics, and stories are all designed to encourage the pleasure of reading.

To order:

Children's Better Health Institute

P.O. Box 7133

Red Oak, IA 51591

515–280–3739

Kid City (Ages 6–10)

The enjoyment of reading is fostered through stories, poems, puzzles, games, and interesting activities ranging from animals and nature to space travel and outer space.

To order:

Children's Television Workshop

P.O. Box 53349

Boulder, CO 80322

800–678–0613

Kids Discover (Ages 6–12)

With emphasis on motivating children to read and write, each issue is devoted to a single theme that lets children discover the world around them.

To order:

Kids Discover

170 Fifth Avenue

New York, NY 10010

212–242–5133

Ladybug, the Magazine for Young Children (Ages 2–7)
Read-aloud and other stories, poems, nursery rhymes, games, songs, and fun activities, all designed to help children experience the pleasure of good literature.
To order:
Carus Publishing
P.O. Box 593
Mt. Morris, IL 61054–0593
800–827–0227

Let's Find Out (Ages 3–6)
A classroom resource that concentrates on current events around the world for preschool and kindergarten children. Includes "Discovery Cards," materials for the teacher, and a take-home letter for parents.
To order:
Scholastic, Inc.
P.O. Box 3710
Jefferson City, MI 65102
800–325–6149

New Moon: The Magazine for Girls and Their Dreams (Ages 8–14)
The contributors are all girls between ages 8 and 14, making this magazine of special interest to this age group. There are short stories, nonfiction articles, and a number of encouraging advice columns.
To order:
New Moon: The Magazine for Girls and Their Dreams
P.O. Box 3587
Duluth, MN 55803
218–728–5507

Ranger Rick (Ages 6–12)
A magazine about nature and the environment, and the appreciation of nature and the environment. Interesting features about natural history, as well as jokes, riddles, plays, and craft ideas. An extra bonus is membership in the Ranger Rick Nature Club.
To order:
National Wildlife Federation
89–25 Leesburg Pike
Vienna, VA 22184–0001
703–790–4000

Scienceland (Ages 5–10)
Fosters scientific thinking in children in picture book format of interest to the very young as well as to older children beginning to understand scientific thinking.
To order:
Scienceland, Inc.
501 Fifth Avenue, Suite 2108
New York, NY 10017–6102
212–490–2180

Sesame Street Magazine (Ages 2–6)
The alphabet, numbers, and problems are introduced along with child-centered activities and games through the characters of the popular television program. Included is a guide for parents that offers suggestions and strategies on child development and parenting skills.
To order:
Children's Television Workshop
P.O. Box 55518
Boulder, CO 80322–1177
800–678–0613

Sports Illustrated for Kids (Ages 8 & Up)
Sports-oriented children are made familiar with outstanding athletes and their stories. Other sections include sports cards, puzzles, and activities.
To order:
Sports Illustrated for Kids
P.O. Box 830609
Birmingham, AL 35283–0609
800–334–2229

Stone Soup: The Magazine for Children (Ages 6–13)
Devoted to art and writing by young children around the world, this literacy magazine touches on a variety of topics related to children's lives. Included are original stories, poetry, and book reviews.
To order:
Children's Art Foundation
P.O. Box 83
Santa Cruz, CA 95063
800–447–4569

Surprises: Activities for Today's Kids and Parents (Ages 5–12)
The magazine's motto is "Learning by Doing." Children are encouraged through active learning activities to learn while having fun.
To order:
Children's Surprises, Inc.
1200 North 7th Street
Minneapolis, MN 55411
612–521–2185

3–2–1 Contact (Ages 8–12)
Geared to interest young scientists, this magazine includes articles about science, math, nature, sociology, computer programming, and psychology.
To order:
Children's Television Workshop
P.O. Box 53051
Boulder, CO 80322–1177
800–678–0613

Turtle Magazine for Preschool Kids (Ages 2–5)
Lots of stories, poems, puzzles, and activities, mainly aimed at meeting the developmental and health needs of young children.
To order:
Children's Better Health Institute
P.O. Box 7133
Red Oak, IA 51591–0133
515–280–3739

U.S. Kids (Ages 5–10)
Fitness and good health practices are highlighted through articles, games, puzzles, and stories about interesting children around the country.
To order:
Children's Better Health Institute
P.O. Box 7133
Red Oak, IA 51591–0133
515–280–3739

Your Big Backyard (Ages 4–8)
Published by the National Wildlife Federation, this magazine,

through stories and activities, helps young children appreciate nature and the importance of conservation.
To order:
National Wildlife Federation
89–25 Leesburg Pike
Vienna, VA 22184–0001
703–790–4000

Zillions for Kids from Consumer Reports (Ages 8–12)
Young children discover how to be informed and critical consumers by learning how best to complain about inferior products and how to evaluate ads and advertising. Teams of children are involved in rating shows, grocery products, school supplies, and just about anything of interest to children.
To order:
Zillions for Kids from Consumer Reports
Subscription Department
P.O. Box 51777
Boulder, CO 80323
800–234–1645

Book Clubs for Children
Children's Book-of-the-Month Club
Customer Service Center
Camp Hill, PA 17012
800–233–0110
800–348–7134 (enrollment line)

Children's Choice Book Club
P.O. Box 938
Hicksville, NY 11802
or Newbridge Communications, Inc.
333 East 38th Street
New York, NY 10016
212–455–5000

Early Start Book Club
P.O. Box 938
Hicksville, NY 11802

or Newbridge Communications, Inc.
333 East 38th Street
New York, NY 10016
212–455–5000

Gateway to Imagination Book Club
P.O. Box 5031
Livermore, CA 94551
800–426–4777
Scholastic Book Clubs
800–325–6149
Books from Scholastic Book Clubs are available only through schools. Ask your child's teacher about Scholastic Book Clubs or make a suggestion to the teacher to sign up the class and/or school for age-appropriate Scholastic Book Clubs including:

1. Firefly (infants and preschoolers through age 5)
2. Seesaw (kindergarten and first grade)
3. The Lucky (second and third grade)
4. Arrow (fourth, fifth, and sixth grade)
5. Tab (seventh, eighth, and ninth grade)

Sesame Street Book Club
P.O. Box 5218
Clifton, NJ 07015
800–537–1517

Trumpet Club
P.O. Box 6003
Columbia, MO 65205
800–826–0110

Weekly Reader Children's Book Club
P.O. Box 16556
Columbus, Ohio 43216
800–456–8220

Books about Children's Reading: A Sampling

Beginning in Whole Language: A Practical Guide. By Kristin G. Schlosser and Vicki L. Phillips. New York: Scholastic, 1991.

Best of the Best for Children. By American Library Association. Edited by Denise Perry Donavin. New York: Random House, 1992.

Beyond Picture Books: A Guide to First Readers. Second Edition. By Barbara Barstow and Judith Riggle. New Providence, N.J.: Bowker, 1995.

Black Authors and Illustrators of Children's Books: A Biographical Dictionary. Second Edition. By Barbara Rollock. New York: Garland, 1992.

The Black Experience in Children's Literature. Selected by The New York Public Library. New York: The New York Public Library, 1994.

Books for Children to Read Alone: A Guide for Parents and Librarians. By George Wilson and Joyce Moss. New York: Bowker, 1988.

Books for the Gifted Child. By Barbara Holland Baskin and Karen H. Harris. Vols. 1 & 2. New York: Bowker, 1980/1988.

Children and Books. Ninth Edition. By Zena Sutherland. New York: Addison Wesley Longman, 1997.

Children's Books: Awards and Prizes. By Children's Book Council. New York: Children's Book Council, 1996.

Children's Books, 1911–1986: Favorite Children's Books from the Branch Collections. Selected by the children's librarians on The New York Public Library staff. New York: The New York Public Library, 1986.

Children's Books: 100 Titles for Reading and Sharing. By the Office of Children's Services. New York: The New York Public Library. (annual).

Children's Literature in the Elementary School. Sixth Edition. By Charlotte S. Huck, et al. Madison, Wisc.: Brown & Benchmark, 1997.

Creative Fingerplays and Action Rhymes: An Index and Guide to Their Use. By Jess Defty. Illustrated by Ellen Kae Hester. Phoenix, Ariz.: Oryx, 1992.

E for Environment: An Annotated Bibliography of Children's Books with Environmental Themes. By Patti K. Sinclair. New Providence, N.J.: Bowker, 1992.

Early Literacy. The Developing Child Series. By Joan Brooks McLane and Gillian Dowley McNamee. Cambridge, Mass.: Harvard University Press, 1990.

Emerging Literacy: Young Children Learn to Read and Write. Edited by Dorothy S. Strickland and Lesley Mandel Morrow. Newark, Del.: International Reading Association, 1989.

Family Literacy: Young Children Learning to Read and Write. By Denny Taylor. Portsmouth, N.H.: Heinemann, 1983.

Family Storybook Reading. By Denny Taylor and Dorothy S. Strickland. Portsmouth, N.H.: Heinemann, 1986.

First Steps toward Reading. By the Editors of Time-Life Books. Alexandria, Va.: Time-Life Books, 1987.

Games for Learning. By Peggy Kaye. New York: Farrar, Straus & Giroux, 1991.

Games for Reading: Playful Ways to Help Your Child Read. By Peggy Kaye. New York: Pantheon Books, 1984.

Games for Writing: Playful Ways to Help Your Child Learn to Write. By Peggy Kaye. New York: Noonday Press, 1995.

Get Ready to Read. By Toni S. Gould. Illustrated by Jo Fahrenkopf. New York: Walker, 1991.

Growing Up Literate: Learning from Inner City Families. By Denny Taylor and Catherine Dorsey-Gaines. Portsmouth, N.H.: Heinemann, 1988.

A Guide to Children's Books about Asian Americans. By Barbara Blake. Brookfield, Vt..: Ashgate Publishing, 1995.

Guidelines to Teaching Remedial Reading: A Holistic Approach. Third Edition. By Lillie Pope. New York: Book Lab, 1996.

Independence in Reading. Third Edition. By Don Holdaway. New York: Ashton Scholastic, 1990.

Language and Literacy in Early Childhood Education. Vols.1–5. Edited by Bernard Spodek and Olivia N. Saracho. New York: Teachers College Press, 1993.

Learning to Read in the '90s. By Roger Young. Berkeley, Calif.: Celestial Arts, 1992.

Literature and the Child. Third Edition. By Bernice E. Cullinan and Lee Galda. San Diego: Harcourt Brace Jovanovich, 1994.

Magazines for Young People: A Children's Magazine Guide. Companion Volume. Second Edition. By Bill Katz and Linda Sternberg Katz. New Providence, N.J.: Bowker, 1991.

More Than the ABC's: The Early Stages of Reading and Writing. By Judith A. Schickedanz. Washington, D.C.: National Association for the Education of Young Children, 1986.

New Treasury of Children's Poetry: Old Favorites and New Discoveries. Selected and introduced by Joanna Cole. Illustrated by Judith Gwyn Brown. Garden City, N.Y.: Doubleday, 1984.

Parents Who Love Reading, Kids Who Don't: How It Happens and What You Can Do about It. By Mary Leonhardt. New York: Crown, 1993.

Preparing Your Child for Reading: A Book of Games. By Brandon Sparkman and Jane Saul. New York: Schocken Books, 1978.

Purchasing an Encyclopedia: Twelve Points to Consider. Fifth Edition. Edited by Sandy Whiteley. Chicago: Booklist, American Library Association, 1996.

Raising a Reader: Make Your Child a Reader for Life. by Paul Kropp. New York: Doubleday, 1993.

The Read-Aloud Handbook. Fourth Edition. By Jim Trelease. New York: Penguin Books, 1995.

Read to Me: Raising Kids Who Love to Read. By Bernice E. Cullinan. New York: Scholastic, 1992.

Reference Books for Children's Collections. Revised Edition. Compiled by the Children's Reference Committee, Office of Children's Services. Edited by Dolores Vogliano. New York: The New York Public Library, 1996.

Resources for Early Childhood: A Handbook. Edited by Hannah Nuba, et al. New York: Garland, 1994.

The RIF Guide to Encouraging Young Readers. Edited by Ruth Granes. New York: Doubleday, 1987.

Sing a Song of Popcorn: Every Child's Book of Poems. Selected by Beatrice Schenk de Regniers, et al. New York: Scholastic, 1988.

Stories: A List of Stories to Tell and Read Aloud. Eighth Edition. Edited by Marilyn Berg Iarusso. New York: The New York Public Library, 1990.

Storytelling: Art and Technique. Third Edition. By Ellin Greene. New Providence, N.J.: Bowker, 1996.

Teach a Child to Read with Children's Books. By Mark B. Thogmartin. Bloomington, Ind.: ERIC Clearinghouse on Reading, English and Communication, 1996.

Teaching Reading to Every Child. Third Edition. By Diane Lapp and James Flood. New York: Macmillan, 1992.

Teaching Them to Read. Sixth Edition. By Dolores Durkin. Boston: Allyn and Bacon, 1993.

This Land Is Our Land: A Guide to Multicultural Literature for Children and Young Adults. By Alethea K. Helbig and Agnes Regan Perkins. Westport, Conn.: Greenwood, 1994.

Three Voices: A Guide to Poetry across the Curriculum. By Bernice E. Cullinan. Columbus, Ohio: Stenhouse Publications, 1995.

Understanding Reading: A Psycholinguistic Analysis of Reading and Learning to Read. Fifth Edition. By Frank Smith. Hillsdale, N.J.: Lawrence Erlbaum Associates, 1994.

Understanding Whole Language: From Principles to Practice. By Constance Weaver. Portsmouth, N.H.: Heinemann, 1990.

Writing to Read: A Parent's Guide to the New, Early Learning Program for Children. By John Henry Martin and Ardy Friedberg. New York: Warner Books, 1986.

Magazines for Parents and Educators

American Baby Magazine
249 West 17th Street
New York, NY 10011
Features articles on pregnancy, health, nutrition, first-year first aid, and other helpful advice for soon-to-be and new parents. Every issue includes a "Dear Parents" column, "Crib Notes," and "Booklets and samples to send for."

Baby Talk/Parenting
301 Howard Street
San Francisco, CA 94105
These "sister" publications offer outstanding advice to parents, each with a somewhat different focus. *Baby Talk* concentrates on the new baby from birth through age two. *Parenting* covers the ages and stages of the child from birth through age eight.

Black Child
P.O. Box 12048
Atlanta, GA 30355
New bimonthly for African-American parents with children up to age ten. Covers social and family issues from the perspective of black culture and history, including child care, education, finances, food, entertainment, travel, and careers.

Childhood Education
Journal of the Association for Childhood Education International
11501 Georgia Avenue
Wheaton, MD 20902
Topics cover childhood education from infancy through early adolescence with thought-provoking, seminal articles for professionals as well as parents.

Early Childhood News
P.O. Box 49728
Dayton, OH 45449
As "the Journal of Professional Development," this publication offers relevant guidelines for professional growth to students and teachers in the field of early education.

Early Childhood Today
Scholastic, Inc.
555 Broadway
New York, NY 10012
The goal of this professional magazine is to support and encourage teachers, directors, and supervisors, and to help them expand their programs through outstanding articles, reports, and tips for strategies to apply in the early childhood classroom. Developing life skills through play, fostering self-esteem, and enriching the classroom environment are some of the features designed to help the educator be optimally successful in their work.

Exceptional Parent
300 Harvard Street
Brookline, MA 02146
This magazine is geared to families and professionals who live or work with children with special needs. Articles featured are most helpful and sensitive.

Mothering
P.O. Box 1690
Santa Fe, NM 87504
Supportive of both parents and children, and seeking to inspire a recognition of the vital importance of parenthood, the magazine is committed to offering the best information available through which parents can make informed decisions about the needs and rights of their children.

Parent and Preschooler Newsletter
Preschool Publications
P.O. Box 1167
Cutchogue, NY 11935
An international resource for professionals and parents, this excellent newsletter offers an extraordinary amount of valuable information in a small package.

Parents
685 Third Avenue
New York, NY 10017

Another excellent magazine for parents of children from birth through age ten. Articles in additon to those on parenting skills offer advice on beauty and fashion for the mother as well as cooking ideas and the latest on children's entertainment, books, music, videos, and movies.

The Reading Teacher
International Reading Association
P.O. Box 8139
Newark, DE 19714
The Reading Teacher is an outstanding professional periodical, published by the International Reading Association. Included are articles, essays, and research summaries on reading and literacy education, as well as classroom ideas, poetry, reviews of children's books, and stories seen through children's eyes.

Sesame Street Parents/Padres de Sesame
Children's Television Workshop
1 Lincoln Plaza
New York, NY 10023
Published by the Children's Television Workshop, this popular magazine offers practical tips on parenting, travel, entertainment, and reviews of children's books, as well as the latest in computer software for children. *Padres de Sesame* is the Spanish-language version of *Sesame Street Parents* magazine, designed as a resource for Spanish-speaking parents whose children are enthusiastic *Sesame Street* fans. The magazine covers the areas of nutrition, safety, education, and activities for infants through grade-school-aged children.

Working Mother
230 Park Avenue
New York, NY 10169
Designed to help mothers successfully balance home and workplace. Articles deal with problems such as having to miss the child's school performance because of work, or how to get a company to provide time for emergency child care. Also features child-rearing advice, software suggestions, and beauty, health, and nutrition guidelines.

Young Children
The Journal of the National Association for the Education of Young
Children
1509 16th Street, NW
Washington, DC 20036
Offers professional development guidelines for early childhood educators working with children from birth through age eight. Outstanding articles and essays by leading educators and child-care practitioners.

Resource Organizations

American Association of School Librarians
50 East Huron Street
Chicago, IL 60611

American Federation of Teachers
555 New Jersey Avenue, NW
Washington, DC 20001

American Library Association
50 East Huron Street
Chicago, IL 60611

Association for Childhood Education International
11141 Georgia Avenue, Suite 200
Wheaton, MD 20902

Association for Supervision and Curriculum Development
1250 North Pitt Street
Alexandria, VA 22314

Children's Book Council
568 Broadway
New York, NY 10012

Children's Defense Fund
25 East E Street, NW
Washington, DC 20001

International Reading Association
800 Barksdale Road
P.O. Box 8139
Newark, DE 19714–8139

National Association for the Education of Young Children
1834 Connecticut Avenue, NW
Washington, DC 20009

National Black Child Development Institute
1023 15th Street, NW, Suite 600
Washington, DC 20005

National Center for Family Literacy
Waterfront Plaza
325 West Main Street, Suite 200
Louisville, KY 40202

National Center for Learning Disabilities
381 Park Avenue South, Suite 1420
New York, NY 10016

National Council on Disability
1331 F Street, NW, Suite 1050
Washington, DC 20004

National Council of Teachers of English
1111 Kenyon Road
Urbana, IL 61801

National Parent–Teacher Association
700 North Rush Street
Chicago, IL 60611

Reading Is Fundamental
600 Maryland Avenue, SW, Suite 600
Washington, DC 20024

Reading Reform Foundation
33 West 57th Street, Suite 1L
New York, NY 10019

The New York Public Library
Central Children's Room at Donnell Library Center
20 West 53rd Street
New York, NY 10019
212–621–0636

Early Childhood Resource and Information Center
66 Leroy Street
New York, NY 10014
212–929–0815

The New York Public Library for the Performing Arts
40 Lincoln Center Plaza
New York, NY 10023
212–870–1630

Children's Rooms at The New York Public Library
Ethnic Heritage Centers
Belmont Library/Enrico Fermi Cultural Center
610 East 186th Street
Bronx, NY 10458
718–933–6410
(Italian Culture)

Chatham Square Regional Library
33 East Broadway
New York, NY 10002
212–964–6598
(Chinese and Chinese-American Culture)

Countee Cullen Regional Library
104 West 136th Street
New York, NY 10030
212–491–2070
(African-American Culture)

Hunt's Point Regional Library
877 Southern Blvd.
Bronx, NY 10459
718–617–0338
(Puerto Rican and Hispanic Culture)

In addition to The New York Public Library listings above, there are
equally fine libraries serving adults and children all over the country.

Chapter Twelve
Postscript

Hannah Nuba
Deborah Lovitky Sheiman
Michael Searson

There is a saying that children who read succeed, and children who succeed read. In the opinion of the editors there could not be truer words. In the past pages we have shown the importance of books to children from birth through age eight. Although the early childhood years have been the focus of this book, we emphasize reading as a lifelong endeavor. There is little in life that can open up as many new experiences, give as much comfort, and bring as much joy as a good book. From parents reading to their babies, to children reading silently to themselves, to adults continuing their reading, good books can provide a satisfying experience.

The adventures in literature described here may differ in types and in areas of interest. However, they do not differ in quality. The many books mentioned throughout this book are only a sampling of the thousands of excellent children's books available. To have put forth an inclusive listing would have been a burdensome task and overwhelming to the reader. Beyond the many reading suggestions offered in *Children's Literature: Developing Good Readers,* libraries and good bookstores offer lists of award-winning books and classics based on age levels and topics of interest.

Similarly, we have tried to emphasize that a good book has dimensions a reader may not be aware of. Authors each have their own personal reasons for putting words to paper. Illustrators all have their own concepts of what they want to create. To have written a book on children's literature and not to have considered these separate but coterminous viewpoints would have made for an incomplete presentation. Every story is told through multiple perspectives—the words of the author, the eyes of the illustrator, the intonations of the storyteller, and the perceptions of the reader.

The books we read to children grow with them. They are the extra pair of eyes that help us look within ourselves and illuminate our dreams and experiences. The effects upon us of a book are not always readily predictable. However, the impact of a good book can last a lifetime. We salute the writers, illustrators, publishers, and readers of children's literature. They are giving the gifts of literacy and pleasure to millions of children across our nation. To help spread these gifts, proceeds from this book are being donated to The New York Public Library.

Contributors

Christine Baykowski majored in early childhood education at Montclair University, Montclair, New Jersey, and received her Bachelor of Arts degree in 1990. She earned her master's degree from Kean University, Union, New Jersey, in 1997, specializing in early childhood education/administration. She has been teaching for eight years and is currently a first-grade teacher in the Rahway, New Jersey, public school system.

Cari Best is the recipient of the 1995 Ezra Jack Keats Award for her first book *Taxi! Taxi!*. Ms. Best, a former children's librarian, is now editorial director at Weston Woods, a film studio specializing in the animation of outstanding children's books. Her own books for Orchard Books include *Taxi! Taxi!; Red Light, Green Light, Mama and Me; Getting Used to Harry; Top Banana;* and *Montezuma's Revenge* (forthcoming); and for DK Inc. *Last Licks: A Story About a Legendary Little Pink Ball* and *Three Cheers for Catherine the Great.*

Hannah Nuba is presently program coordinator of the New York Public Library Early Childhood Resource and Information Center (ECRIC). She holds a master's degree, summa cum laude, from Columbia University, and has done doctoral studies in child development at New York University. She also holds certification in early childhood education and library science from the State University of New York and a degree in educational psychology from Goddard College in Vermont. She is an elected member of Beta Phi Mu, the International Library Honor Society. Ms. Nuba developed and implemented ECRIC, the New York Public Library's pioneering program in library service that has attracted worldwide attention in the early childhood education and library communities and redefined the way libraries serve children from birth to age eight and the adults who care for them. Ms. Nuba's column "Children's Bookshelf" appeared regularly in *Ladies' Home Journal Parents Digest*, and she is a member of the Advisory Panel to Children's Television Workshop's Family Living Series, published by Prentice Hall. Among her publications are *Resources for Early Childhood: A Handbook* (Garland Publishing) and *Infants: Research and Resources* (Teachers College Press). Ms. Nuba's forthcoming publication is *Books! Books! Books! Developing Active Readers in the Early Childhood Classroom*, published by Childcraft Education Corporation.

Siobhan O'Neil, who graduated from the New School for Social Research, Eugene Lang College, is assistant to Hannah Nuba, program coordinator of the New York Public Library Early Childhood Resource and Information Center. She is executive director of the Yemaya Corporation, a nonprofit organization providing far-reaching family support programs. She is an active member of the Catholic Worker, a pacifist Christian community, and a contributor to the *Catholic Worker* newspaper.

Anita Riggio is the award-winning writer/illustrator of a number of picture books, including *Secret Signs,* a 1997 Society of School Librarians International Honor Book; *Beware the Brindlebeast,* a 1995 Parents' Choice Silver Honor Book; and the much-beloved Christmas story, *A Moon in My Teacup.* She is the illustrator of many other picture books, most notably *Coal Mine Peaches* by Michelle Dionetti, a 1993 NCSS-CBC Notable Children's Trade Book, and *The Whispering Cloth,* a 1996 IRA Teachers' Choice, NCTE Notable Children's Book, and NCSS-CBC Notable Trade Book. Ms. Riggio has studied writing with Jacqueline Woodson, Brock Cole, and Chris Lynch. In January 1999, she will receive an MFA in Writing for Children from Vermont College of Norwich University. She is currently completing her first novel for young adult readers.

Michael Searson is Professor of Early Childhood and Family Studies at Kean University, New Jersey. He teaches curriculum, child development, and educational technology at the graduate and undergraduate levels. He holds a Ph.D. in Cognitive Studies and Child Development from Rutgers University. Additionally, he taught preschool children and kindergartners for six years in New York City.

Deborah Lovitky Sheiman, who holds a doctorate in education, has been an educational consultant in child development and education for the past thirty years. She has taught in the classroom and university, counseled families and children, started child development centers, and initiated resource programs in public education. She has testified before congressional committees in support of child welfare and was adjunct faculty at the University of Connecticut for eleven years. Dr. Sheiman has contributed child development articles to professional publications and compendiums. She is the co-editor of *Resources for Early Childhood: A Handbook* and co-author of *Infancy: A Guide to Research and Resources* and *Resources for Middle Childhood: A Source Book.*

Jill Renee Sheiman graduated from the University of Michigan and is currently pursuing graduate studies at Northwestern University. She has worked as a research assistant and as a field study assistant. She has written articles on both psychology and education. She is the co-author of "Early Childhood Education Tools: Organizations, Periodicals and Databases" in *Resources for Early Childhood: A Handbook.*

Laura Suzanne Sheiman is a student at Cornell University. She has worked as a research assistant in child development. Her publishing credits include co-authoring the chapter "Early Childhood Education Tools: Organizations, Periodicals and Databases" in *Resources for Early Childhood: A Handbook.*

Nicole Vogel has been teaching first grade for four years in the Linden, New Jersey, public school system. She graduated from Kean University, Union, New Jersey in 1993 with a Bachelor of Arts degree in early childhood education and received her master's degree in early childhood education/administration from Kean University in 1997.

Source Books on Education

MULTICULTURAL EDUCATION
A Source Book
by Patricia G. Ramsey,
Edwina B. Vold,
and Leslie R. Williams

RELIGIOUS HIGHER EDUCATION
IN THE UNITED STATES
A Source Book
edited by Thomas C. Hunt
and James C. Carper

TEACHERS AND MENTORS
*Profiles of Distinguished
Twentieth-Century Professors
of Education*
edited by Craig Kridel,
Robert V. Bullough, Jr.,
and Paul Shaker

MULTICULTURALISM IN
ACADEME
A Source Book
by Libby V. Morris
and Sammy Parker

AT-RISK YOUTH
Theory, Practice, Reform
by Robert F. Kronick

RELIGION AND SCHOOLING
IN CONTEMPORARY AMERICA
*Confronting Our
Cultural Pluralism*
edited by Thomas C. Hunt
and James C. Carper

K–12 CASE STUDIES
FOR SCHOOL ADMINISTRATORS
Problems, Issues, and Resources
by Marcia M. Norton
and Paula E. Lester

CHILDREN'S LITERATURE
Developing Good Readers
edited by Hannah Nuba,
Deborah Lovitky Sheiman,
and Michael Searson

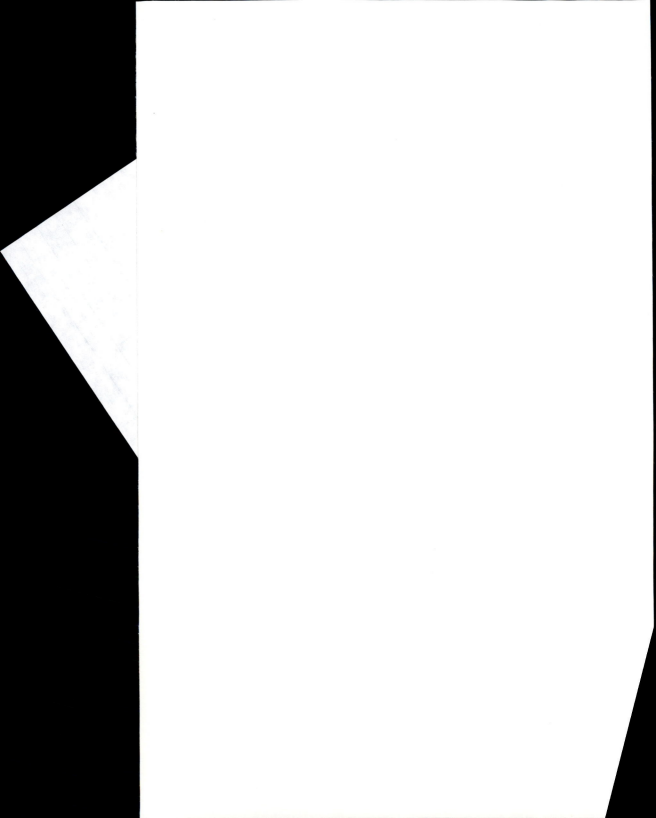

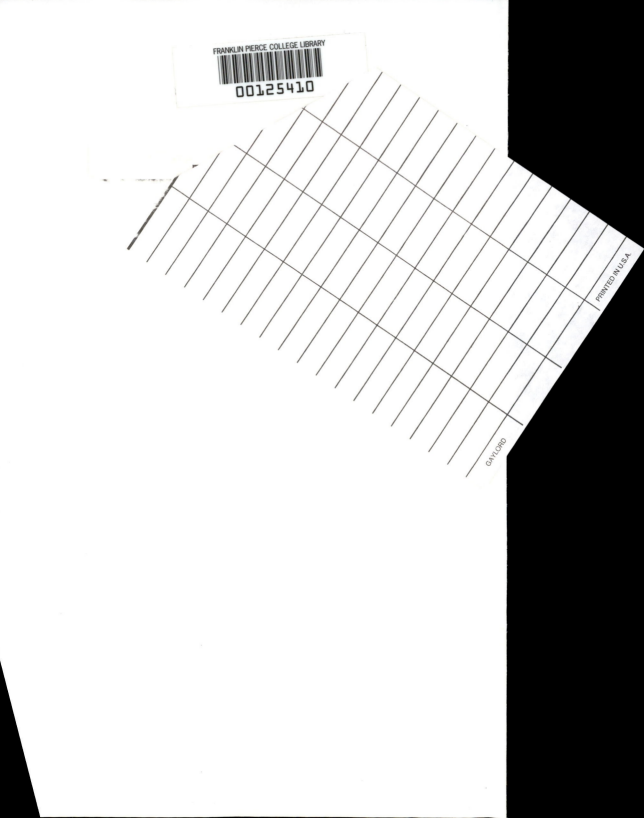